FINDING YOUR COSTA RICA

5 Powerful Steps to Personal, Professional and Financial Success.

Dr. TIMOTHY A. LASKIS

Order this book online at www.trafford.com/07-0002
or email orders@trafford.com

Most Trafford titles are also available at major online book retailers.

© Copyright 2007 Timothy Laskis

All rights reserved. No part of this publication may be reproduced, stored in a retrieval system, or transmitted, in any form or by any means, electronic, mechanical, photocopying, recording, or otherwise, without the written prior permission of the author.

Note for Librarians: A cataloguing record for this book is available from Library and Archives Canada at www.collectionscanada.ca/amicus/index-e.html

ISBN: 978-1-4251-1525-8

We at Trafford believe that it is the responsibility of us all, as both individuals and corporations, to make choices that are environmentally and socially sound. You, in turn, are supporting this responsible conduct each time you purchase a Trafford book, or make use of our publishing services. To find out how you are helping, please visit www.trafford.com/responsiblepublishing.html

Our mission is to efficiently provide the world's finest, most comprehensive book publishing service, enabling every author to experience success. To find out how to publish your book, your way, and have it available worldwide, visit us online at www.trafford.com/10510

www.trafford.com

North America & international
toll-free: 1 888 232 4444 (USA & Canada)
phone: 250 383 6864 ♦ fax: 250 383 6804
email: info@trafford.com

The United Kingdom & Europe
phone: +44 (0)1865 722 113 ♦ local rate: 0845 230 9601
facsimile: +44 (0)1865 722 868 ♦ email: info.uk@trafford.com

10 9 8 7 6 5 4

ACKNOWLEDGMENTS

To my wife, Isabel, you are the light in my life. The wisdom I have gained from you is priceless. Te Amo.

To my parents, David and Jayne, I am truly grateful for all your love and support. You believed in me before I believed in myself, and I can't thank you enough.

To my brother Jon Paul, You always remind me how important it is to have fun. Love ya man.

To Dr. Kerri Chase, I appreciate your time spent editing and your support over the years.

To all my friends and colleagues, your words of encouragement always strengthened me and propelled me forward. I am grateful to have you in my life.

CONTENTS

PART ONE
The Right Path 9

Chapter One
It's About Choice 11

Chapter Two
Myths of Success 31

Chapter Three
My Story of Overcoming Obstacles 41

PART TWO
The Life You Always Wanted 49

Chapter Four
Step One: Focus on Passion 51

Chapter Five
Step Two: Create a Plan 63

Chapter Six
Step Three: Think Positive 75

Chapter Seven
Step Four: Be Persistent 91

Chapter Eight
Step Five: Live with Purpose. 103

PART THREE
Powerful Outcomes **113**

Chapter Nine
A Picture of a Successful Journey 115

Chapter Ten
The Next Step 123

Chapter Eleven
My Thoughts to You 131

Index **135**

PART ONE

THE RIGHT PATH

CHAPTER ONE

IT'S ABOUT CHOICE

"Your own resolution to succeed is more important than any other one thing." – Abraham Lincoln

Here I sit on a white sandy beach in exotic Costa Rica with a warm ocean breeze in my face and sounds of monkeys playing in the jungle. The best part of all: it's not a dream and I'm not on vacation—I live here. I left my cozy job with the state of California to seek adventure in Costa Rica. Colleagues and friends told me I was crazy to leave a secure job. They said it was a gamble to do so, reminding me that if I continued to work for the state, I would be set for life with good benefits and a pension. However, it was a bigger gamble in my opinion to be tied to a job I no longer enjoyed; I didn't want to just wait for retirement, hoping I would have a few years of good health to follow my dreams.

Well over a year ago my brother and I took our first trip to Costa Rica. Our desire to surf some of the best waves in the world led us here. However, this trip turned out to be much more than a surfing adventure; as it changed my life forever.

On our first day, while eating at a local restaurant, I saw the most stunning young lady sitting at the next table. She had gorgeous long black hair, tan skin, and a beautiful smile. I immediately leaned over and said, "Hi, my name is Tim, are you from here?" I was extremely nervous, and as quickly as she first glanced at me, she looked away without responding.

I was persistent, telling her that I lived in California, and this was my first trip to Costa Rica. She nodded but never said a word. On my third attempt she finally said something in Spanish. At that moment I realized she did not speak English and had not understood a word I said. I felt foolish, and then I quickly recalled some bits of Spanish I'd learned in high school. Que hora es, I said with a slow southern twang. She looked at me and laughed and said her name was Isabel.

For several hours we used a primitive form of sign language to communicate. We really enjoyed each other's company and decided to walk to the dance club down the street. However, once we arrived, we lost each other in the crowd. I never had a chance to talk or dance with her. Just as fast as I'd found the woman of my dreams, she disappeared.

For two days and two nights I scoured the area looking for Isabel. The last night before I was to leave town, I returned to the restaurant where we first met. At first I did not see her, but then suddenly she appeared across the room. She walked rapidly over to me and my heart did a flip. I could not have been happier. We used our awkward sign language to communicate as we ate dinner and laughed together. Afterward, we headed to the club where we danced until they closed.

At the end of the night we exchanged telephone numbers and I gave Isabel a quick kiss before saying goodbye. I felt like a schoolboy in love for the first time. As my brother and I drove away I promised myself I would see her again.

A few days after arriving back in California I attempted to contact Isabel by telephone. I knew I couldn't communicate in Spanish but I wanted to hear her voice. However, when I called, someone spoke Spanish very rapidly and hung up. I did not understand what was said and apparently I was not understood. I called a few more times and on each occasion the person spoke about ninety miles per hour and hung up. I was confused and thought I probably had the wrong number.

Two weeks passed without having any luck of contacting her. A friend of mine who speaks Spanish agreed to help. She called the number and found out that Isabel lived down the street, but she did not have a telephone. The woman who answered explained, however, that she would give Isabel my message, and we agreed that I would call back the next day at 5:00 pm when Isabel could be there to answer my call.

We called the next day as scheduled and Isabel answered the phone. My friend translated and it was great to be in contact. We set up several phone sessions and began using email. She wrote to me in Spanish, and I was able to translate her emails with my friend's help and by using a Spanish-English translation webstite. I studied Spanish day and night, and once I felt comfortable, I began calling her on my own.

I scheduled a trip back to Costa Rica the very next month. I had a wonderful time with Isabel and enjoyed getting to know her unique personality better as well as learning more about her family and culture. We passed the time taking walks on the beach, watching monkeys swing from the trees, and eating fresh fruit. I was convinced she was the woman for me. When I returned to the States we continued to email and talk on the phone weekly and we grew closer with each contact.

Approximately three months from the day I met her, I made a surprise visit and asked her to marry me. She said yes, and I traveled to see her every few weeks until I moved to Costa Rica five months later. Soon after we were married in San Jose, Costa Rica surrounded by our friends and family.

*What a fantastic day we had.
I could not have been any happier.*

This was not the first time in my life I made such a bold decision. Almost seventeen years ago I began my journey of creating a better life for myself. Prior to that I had been on a road to nowhere as I had a poor academic history, low self-esteem, and no career goals. Basically, I had no insight into what I wanted to do, who I wanted to be, or where I wanted to go.

I began examining my life, determining what I needed

to do in order to get ahead and succeed. I knew the journey would not be easy, but the consequence of doing nothing was even more painful. In the end my effort and hard work paid off as I earned a doctorate in clinical psychology, met the woman of my dreams, began working for myself, and now enjoy living in beautiful Costa Rica.

I have helped many people who have struggled to improve their lives, and one factor they've all had in common was negativity. This negative mindset stemmed from their past, present, future or often all three. They were immobilized by their negative thoughts and feelings, with no way of escape. However, this situation is not unique; almost everyone has fallen into this trap at one time or another. I'm sure some of these examples may be familiar to you.

"I want to be happy in my relationship with my wife, but I just don't think I ever will be. I've tried really hard for years without any success. I guess things will never change."

"I've been working hard at my job with hopes of moving up the ladder. However, when a higher position opens up, I never get promoted. Maybe I'm just not meant to work at management level."

"My credit cards are maxed out and I live paycheck to paycheck. I want to make more money, but I wouldn't know where to begin. Unless you are born into a wealthy family, it's almost impossible to be financially secure."

Everyone has the ability to lead a life either of happiness or misery. There is nothing special about those who have successful relationships, stimulating careers or large bank accounts. They are not born with a gene for success and happiness and you are not born with a gene for failure and misery. We are all the same and interconnected. The power I have to change my life is the same power you have. The difference between those who succeed and those who do not is "choice." Those who succeed choose not to sit around and dream for a better life. They choose to make positive changes and not succumb to negativity, whether it's expressed in their thoughts, feelings, or behavior. Falling into the trap of negativity will certainly paralyze you and never allow you to reach your goals and dreams.

EXAMINING YOUR OPTIONS

Clients I have treated who suffered from mental illness coupled with developmental disabilities often had maladaptive behaviors that prevented them from being successful in the community. Many had difficulty managing their emotions when feeling frustrated, angry, or anxious.

As a result, they lashed out verbally or physically resulting in injury to themselves and others. My goal was to help them realize they had a number of options for handling any situation.

For example, if Sammy called Wilson a derogatory name, Wilson could return the favor and curse Sammy, push him, punch him, kick him, walk away, tell Sammy he does not appreciate his behavior, let staff know, talk it over, or just ignore it.

I helped clients recognize all of their options, good and bad, and see the benefits and pitfalls of each. After that, I left it up to them. At that point they were in control.

Empowering clients to see their choices and the consequences of each has been one of the most effective strategies I use in improving the quality of their lives. I know the power of choice because I too discovered many years ago I had a choice to sit on the sidelines of life or get in the game.

Examining the consequences of each option helped me decide what I needed to do. I have come a long way from my youthful beginnings in Greenville, South Carolina. I went from being undisciplined and unmotivated (and almost failing out of high school) to later earning my doctorate.

Many of my friends and relatives were very surprised I had accomplished so much because I had never been identified as one of the "most likely to succeed" individuals. I was not listed as the most popular in my yearbook nor was I noted as a star athlete. My grades were poor, I graduated at the bottom of my high school class and my Standardized Achievement Test (SAT) scores were low.

However, in light of my poor academic history I made a choice not only to be successful but to succeed in academia as well. Just like my clients who were empowered to look at all of their options and examine the consequences of each, I too had the power to look at mine.

If I had chosen to continue on the path of not taking life seriously I would have faced the outcome of that choice. This possibly meant earning low pay, having poor housing, and enjoying few, if any, luxuries in life. Because I chose a different path the outcome was much different. However, this route was not the path of least resistance, nothing came easy.

THREE CHOICES

How many times have you found yourself talking with your spouse, close friend, or co-worker about a dream of yours? Or theirs? Probably many. Listen carefully to the conversations regarding new cars, homes, careers, or exotic vacations. Often someone says, "Yeah, Hawaii must be nice, I wish I could take a vacation there," or, "Wow, look at that new ski boat, I bet they have a lot of fun on the weekend." Then someone mentions how he needs to win the lottery and describes the things he would buy and places he would visit with his new-found fortune.

However, as years go by many people continue to work in the same job, make the same salary, and have the same conversations with everyone about the day they will win the lottery in order to have what they desire.

I saw a television commercial for the California lottery. A man is sitting in traffic looking at his lottery ticket when he notices a yacht being transported on a trailer. The name of the yacht is Jasmine but the first three letters are covered and all he sees is "mine." The commercial ends with a catchy song and a guy singing, "Maybeeee, Maybeeee." It really captures this wonderful experience of dreaming. Everyone does it but when the dream ends you have three options:

1. You can continue dreaming about what others have without actually ever obtaining it.
2. Stop dreaming, accept that you are not fortunate enough to have what others have, and forget about it.
3. Decide that you have not reached your full potential and anything you put your mind to can become reality.

Which option will you choose? Many people put a lot of energy into only dreaming about a better life. Others try hard to push the thoughts away. Of course, neither option will ever get them anywhere. This is analogous to a boat without a propeller. The engine may be running, but it's just not moving. In time the engine dies and the boat continues drifting into the open sea. I don't know about you, but I get tired of "only" dreaming. Dreaming is fine but you have to make a decision to obtain what you want in life. You deserve it just as much as anyone else.

Those who truly believe they can't achieve "better" things in life, waste a considerable amount of effort and energy. They often try to shut out thoughts about getting a better career, a nicer home, more money, or a higher education.

In reality they could actually have achieved their goals with half the energy they used in thinking negatively.

Have you met someone who always makes negative statements about what others have? "Nobody needs to have all that money, that's greedy," or "People who buy expensive cars are just wasting their money." Such remarks maybe a sign that person doesn't believe he can have what others have. Such comments are often laced with negativity and sarcasm. They often emanate from the same individuals who live paycheck to paycheck and work on their car every weekend just to keep it running.

Denis Waitley sums up this style of thinking nicely. "The reason most people never reach their goals is that they don't define them, learn them or ever seriously consider them as believable or achievable." Again, if you don't believe you can achieve something, chances are you never will. This is a self-fulfilling prophecy that will limit you if you allow it.

When I read about people who accomplish amazing feats, I become excited for them. I really feel happy for them, share their joy, and become motivated, because it reaffirms that anything in life can be accomplished. It's like sending a man into space for the first time, once everyone knows it can be done, it just opens the door for more space exploration. If someone else does something I haven't done I become inspired. I believe deep down that I too can accomplish whatever I set my mind to.

However, if you have a belief system that you don't deserve and can't have the best life has to offer, you will simply never have it. My guess is that you are not this person because you picked up this book and have read this far. This is a powerful sign that you are tired of wasting energy "just" dreaming and thinking negatively. You are ready to take the necessary steps in making your dreams a reality!

Robert Lipkin also known as "Bob Bitchin," the founder of Latitudes and Attitudes, (a magazine for those who love sailboats and the cruising lifestyle) once stated, "Don't dream your life, live your dream!" This is a man who does just that. For most of his life he has done what he wanted to do when he wanted to do it.

Lipkin spent nearly 20 years early in his life riding with bikers while writing about the outlaw lifestyle. He founded Biker Magazine and Tattoo Magazine and was an editor for several motorcycle publications. He found a way to make money doing something he enjoyed. And, when his passion for motorcycles lost its kick he traded in his Harley for a sailboat.

Lipkin's next journey took him across the open sea as he became an experienced sailor accumulating more than 75,000 miles of ocean travel. As a result, he started a cruisers magazine titled: Latitudes and Attitudes. His life is spent doing what he is passionate about without the 9 to 5 constraints. How many of us can say that?

It is sad that many people work in jobs they greatly dislike. Day in and day out they continue to sit in a cubicle or office waiting for a week or two of vacation each year. Now, think about this for a moment. If you worked each week Monday thru Friday in 2007 without missing a day you would accumulate 261 days on the job. Let's say you received two weeks of vacation (10 working days). This would mean that you worked 251 days in order to receive only 10 days of vacation! I don't know about you but that doesn't seem like a good deal to me, especially if you are unhappy at your job. But, no matter where you are in your life, you can always choose to turn it around.

BEING READY FOR CHANGE

Our lives are similar to riding a roller coaster with all the ups, downs, twists and turns. Sometimes you hold on for dear life while other times you sit and enjoy the climb. However, on the roller coaster of life you have more control than you think you have. You are not strapped in without an escape or exit. In fact, you have control over which tracks to ride. Deciding to change tracks is the first step. Your commitment to changing your life propels you toward your goals.

Many philosophers, teachers, mental health professionals, and life coaches will tell you that one cannot change unless he or she is ready and willing to. Drug and alcohol programs are full of people who are not ready to stop using harmful substances. They continue to receive treatment either because of court mandate or pressure from family and/or friends. However, many of them will fail repeatedly because deep down they are not ready or committed to changing their behavior. The old adage you can lead a horse to water but you cannot make him drink, rings true.

Over the years I have worked in clinical settings with adolescents and adults who were members of gangs. Along with helping them learn new coping skills for managing their anger or dealing with stress, I also attempted to help them see that the gang lifestyle was a dead-end road. At times it was very difficult as they were resistant and sometimes hostile. Here I was trying to show a pattern of problems that stem from their affiliation with gangs, but I was having little success. The bottom line was until they were ready to adopt a new lifestyle they were not going to change. It was like trying to tear down a brick wall with a toothpick. I knew it was not going to be easy but I kept trying in hopes I would catch them when they were ready.

I took classes for fourteen years before I did well in academics. I had many different teachers who taught various subjects for all those years but I did not do well until I was ready. Nothing was going to make me succeed until I wanted to succeed.

Sitting on the sideline watching everyone else become successful was not what I wanted to do. My options were clear, continue on a path with no real promise or choose a path toward success. The answer for me was easy because I was very unhappy and ready for change. This applies to every area of life either personally, professionally, or financially. Take a moment and answer the following questions using the scale below.

SATISFACTION EXERCISE

Scale: 1   2   3   4   5
       Very   Unhappy Somewhat   Satisfied   Very
     Unhappy   Satisfied   Satisfied

1. On a scale of 1 to 5, how do you rate your personal life (quality of relationships with family and friends and spiritual connection)?

_____

2. On a scale of 1 to 5, how do you rate your professional life (job or career)?

_____

3. On a scale of 1 to 5, how do you rate your financial position (current salary, savings, and amount of personal possessions)?

_____

Once you answer the above questions take some time to look at your ratings. If your scores in any area were 1 or 2 you are ready for change. However, if your scores in any area were 3, you may not be ready. There really needs to be a certain degree of pain or displeasure for change to occur. For example, if you always wanted to be in another field of work but your current job is somewhat satisfying, you may not have the motivation to change.

Even a tiny bit of satisfaction can keep you in your current job. Think of it like placing your hand in a bucket of water. If the water is boiling hot you will jerk your hand away immediately, however, if the water is warm you will keep it in there much longer.

Some of you may find that change is needed in all three areas of your life, while others may have only one or two. Regardless of how bad things are, you are fully capable of turning it around. Now pick either a personal, professional or financial category you want to improve in and answer these questions.

GOAL EXERCISE

1. What are two short-term goals you would like to accomplish within the next five months?

_____

_____

2. What are two long-term goals you would like to accomplish within the next five years?

_____

_____

3. What are the benefits of reaching each of your goals?

_____

_____

4. Will you gain anything if you strive for, but do not immediately succeed in reaching your goals?

The first two questions should get your wheels turning as to what you would like to achieve. Your answer to the third question should clearly describe your motivation for setting out to reach your goals. I often use this exercise when working with people who want to improve their lives.

Many times I get wonderful responses such as obtain a college degree, change jobs, buy a new home, or become a star athlete. Then I direct them to think about the benefits of achieving each goal.

For instance, earning a college degree can make their family proud, build self-esteem, provide more knowledge, enable them to work in a field they enjoy and provide financial stability to raise a family. Earning a college degree in and of itself is not that special. It is the reward that goes along with it that we desire.

On the other hand, you may have been surprised when you read question four, "Will you gain anything if you strive for, but do not immediately succeed in reaching your goals?" Some may respond by stating there is nothing to gain.

Let's use an example to evaluate this further. Suppose one of your goals is to buy a second home to use as rental property. You immediately begin researching homes and learning various methods of buying rental property. You then take a seminar that teaches you financing techniques. At the same time you attempt to save for a down payment. Then you begin searching far and wide for potential deals.

After a year passes you finally find the perfect one. You are excited and begin to imagine what upgrades will be done and what new landscaping would look like. However, when you review your bank statement you find you do not have enough money for a down payment and can't proceed. What have you gained?

For starters, you have more knowledge about buying real estate than when you began. You also know a strategy that does not work for saving money. That's right, you now know a strategy that does not work for saving money. You could go to all your friends and bet them you know a sure-fire method how not to save money.

Now, this may sound ridiculous but it's true. The key is to try a new strategy for saving money. You now know how to buy a second home but you just have to fine-tune your strategy for saving. In the end you have gained a tremendous amount of knowledge on investing in real estate. You have not failed unless you quit.

We all have different goals and dreams and regardless of how big or small they are you can accomplish them. Whether you desire to own your own business, improve your golf game, get in shape, rekindle your relationship with your children, become a more effective CEO, or to be a better husband or wife.

I overcame significant obstacles in developing a relationship with my wife. I did not speak Spanish, knew nothing about her culture, and lived two time zones away. However, I did not let this stand in the way of my love and I worked hard. I made my dreams come true and I found my Costa Rica.

The country of Costa Rica is very beautiful and full of exotic wildlife, plants, and people. It's truly a paradise where you can relax and enjoy life. However, it's also a state of mind. Reaching your goals no matter how big or small can give you the same experience. Your Costa Rica is out there and it's up to you to find it.

Just one of the many beautiful Costa Rican beaches.

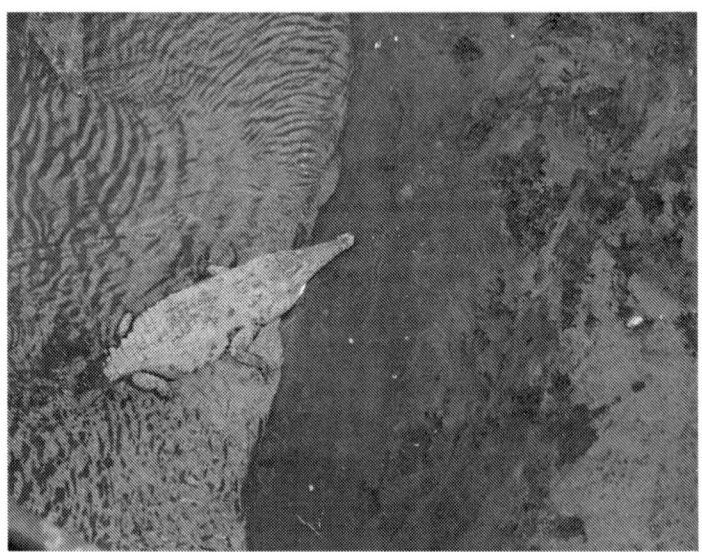

While driving, I noticed several people standing on a bridge looking over the side. This is what they were seeing.

Costa Rica is teaming with wildlife. Here a Capuchin or white-faced monkey enjoys a snack with her baby.

In chapters four through eight you will learn five steps to make any dream a reality. These include connecting with your passion, creating a solid plan of action, thinking positive, utilizing persistence, and living with purpose. Whether you desire personal, business, or financial gains these steps will get you there. However, the first step is to decide whether or not you are dedicated to making the necessary changes. Here are some examples of inner dialogue of those who are ready for change versus those who are not.

Ready: *"Life is too short to work at a job I am no longer passionate about. From this day forward I will work toward my lifelong goal of being self-employed."*

Not Ready: *"Yeah, I don't really enjoy my job but at least it's stable and it pays the bills."*

Ready: "*It is unacceptable to live paycheck to paycheck. I am tired of wearing raggedy clothes, driving old cars and not being able to take trips. I have the ability to make as much money as I want if I put my mind to it.*"

Not Ready: "*I don't like working two low-paying jobs but I'm just not qualified to do anything else. I'm just not meant to have more money.*"

Ready: "*I really love my wife and it is unacceptable to let my work come between us. If I continue on this path we will most likely end in divorce. I will do everything possible from this day forward to show her how much I care.*"

Not Ready: "*It's really difficult juggling my career and my relationship with my wife. I love her but I have to work hard and if she can't accept that then it's her problem.*"

The circumstances of your life aren't always easy to deal with. If you rationalize your problems, difficulties, or pain you will most likely continue to wallow in them. If you decide to change areas you are unhappy with, you will.

This isn't a matter of just saying or thinking positive thoughts, it's about making changes in your core being.

CHAPTER OVERVIEW

- It's your choice to sit on the sidelines or get in the game.
- Decide what areas of your life you want to change and set goals.
- Create a list of benefits for each goal to use as motivation.
- Focus not only on what you have to gain but also what you have to lose by not striving for change.
- Make changes and find your Costa Rica.

CHAPTER TWO

MYTHS
OF
SUCCESS

"If you have faith in yourself you can do anything."
– Spanish Proverb

How many times have you heard someone attempt to explain why they could not get ahead in life?

- Their boss will not promote them.
- Others do not appreciate their work.
- They never had the opportunity to go to college.
- They did not get their break early enough.
- They had bad luck.

These thoughts are not reasons, they are excuses. All the above examples placed responsibility on something or someone else for not doing well in life. It is very easy to look outward for answers instead of inward when analyzing our lives. That is why in psychotherapy, clients are directed to look at themselves more deeply. Regardless of what others do or do not do to us, we ultimately have a choice. No one promotes us to greatness "just because we are special." Nor do they hold us back from being successful. We are solely responsible for our future and the choices we make along the way.

COPING WITH NEGATIVITY THAT SURROUNDS YOU

When you encounter others who do not believe in you, it can make it even more difficult to believe in yourself.

Dealing with family, friends, and even strangers who are negative and pessimistic can be tough. If you encounter those who do not support your goals, understand they have a different belief system. A few weeks ago I was having a conversation with a gentleman about salaries when I told him what I thought I was worth. He immediately looked at me with such disbelief you would have thought I told him I was a leprechaun. Almost instantly while laughing he stated, "You sure are greedy and besides you'll never make that much."

Pondering his response later that day, it made total sense to me. He and I did not share the same beliefs. His belief system is wired very differently and he will make only that amount he believes he deserves. There is nothing wrong with this. It is not my place to tell others how little or how much they should make. That is their decision. Just so, no one can decide for you how much money you should make.

If you find it difficult being around those with negative attitudes try surrounding yourself with those who support you and who bring positive energy with them. However, when you encounter negativity use it as motivation. Turn others' negativity into fuel that fires you up. Use it to propel you further. It's all a matter of how you process your thoughts.

DON'T RESPOND WITH ANGER

On those occasions when you meet people who do not see eye to eye with you on your capabilities or dreams, understand that's only their belief, not truth. The best way to respond is to just talk about it without allowing your ego to get bruised. Don't take it personally. It really isn't a reflection of who you are or aren't. You are the only person responsible for you and no one else can decide whether you succeed or not.

Everyone has a right to believe what he wants and to express his opinion. If you react with anger and hostility, it will only do more harm than good. It really is a waste of energy to take this route. When one reacts with anger it usually means he is not sure of himself. Inside, he questions whether he really has the ability to do what he is so angry about.

If you are sure of yourself you don't need to react in a hostile way. You will benefit much more if you channel your energy working toward your goal instead of wasting it on trying to prove your point. Your point will ultimately be proven when you accomplish what you set out to do. Your behavior and results speak much more clearly than your words.

Working with clients mandated to treatment by the courts because of violent offenses, proved to be very difficult. I came across every excuse in the world for why they assaulted someone. The two most common responses I received were, "They made me do it" or "I didn't have any other choice." I asked how the other person made them do it. "Well if he didn't curse me and disrespect me I wouldn't have punched him."

Some have even stated, "Come on, Doc, you would have done the same thing." I responded, "Yes, I could punch him but I also have other options which lead to better outcomes."

At times it's almost comical to hear new clients rationalize, deny, and blame others. However, sometimes their mindset is such that they don't really see their other choices.

Many people use defense mechanisms such as rationalization, justification, minimization, and blaming to avoid responsibility. Some of these offenders had horrific experiences growing up. A few were beaten quite often for doing any little thing wrong. It was a matter of survival to be quick with an excuse or with a knife in order to save their life. While this does not excuse the behavior, it certainly makes it clear how this maladaptive behavior developed.

Everyone learns early on how to avoid blame. It makes us feel better if outside forces beyond our control cause "terrible" things to happen. I also have used blaming to my advantage. My most memorable experience happened in the fifth grade when I reported to the teacher, "My goat ate my homework." The teacher saw right through this excuse and my fellow students laughed hysterically. It was true I had a goat and that he did indeed ingest my work, however, I was the one who left it outside. Still it felt better to think the "bad" goat was to blame. We all have our escape goats, but just as we rationalize why bad things happen to us, we rationalize why good things happen to others.

Many attribute the good fortune of others to:

- Being lucky
- Having been born into a privileged family
- Having the right connections
- Cheating

While this may be partly true for some, many other factors account for success. Thinking that only luck, birth-right, selling your soul to the devil, or any other force outside of you is the only way to "have it all" is just a cop out.

Having a belief system that our success or failure rests in the hands of others is just not accurate. It is true that those we meet can help us along the way to achieve our goals and dreams. However, the process of reaching the end result does not rest on this premise alone. The process begins with making a choice to strive for your goals.

The five steps covered in the next several chapters are the key ingredients that help you along the way. These principles for success and self-empowerment will show you how to reach any goal by only focusing on one person, you. You are the only one responsible for your success. I believe strongly that everyone has the ability to achieve anything they dream up. Goals you do not accomplish should not be blamed on your parents, teachers, coach, wife, husband, boss, banker, talent agent, publisher, or the devil. Your success and failure ultimately rests in your hands.

I would never have reached my goals if I made excuses or waited around for something good to happen. I attended many schools where teachers and professors did not believe in me. I knew they thought I was not the "crème de la crème" because I received little attention except to be corrected for talking out of turn. I cannot count how many times I sat in the back of my classes feeling miserable and stupid. For a while I did whine, complain, and tell everyone that my teachers were terrible and the standardized tests were unfair. However, no amount of sympathy was going to change things. No one was going to give me a high-paying job because they felt sorry for me. To this day I would still be sitting around waiting for the charity train if it were not for my decision to change my life.

Alfred Adler, a psychiatrist who at one time worked closely with Sigmond Freud, developed a theory of motivation. He postulated that every human being is driven by a force to strive for perfection. Everyone works constantly to fulfill their potential. His theory places success on the individual's innate drive, which further supports the notion that success is not external but rather an internal process.

Just remember success is never handed out. There are no specific groups of people who control successful outcomes of others. At times you may find yourself surrounded by those who do not understand your drive or ambitions. However, it makes no difference whether they support you or not.

When discussing my plans to buy property in Costa Rica many of my friends and family told me not to do it. They said it was risky, foolish, and I did not know what I was doing. At that point I had several options. I could have agreed and not bought it, told them they were crazy, ignored them, or stated I appreciated their concern but this is a goal I plan to reach.

We always have options in which to choose. Regardless of what others say or do you ultimately are responsible for your life. I thanked my loved ones for being concerned about me buying property in Costa Rica however, I was going to obtain my goal. Several months later, I successfully bought 12 beautiful acres in the mountains with rolling pasture, lush rainforest, waterfalls, and sweeping city views.

Standing on top of my property looking into the valley below. The air is always brisk and clean here.

This is a view to the other side of the property.

Isabel poses by a tree we discovered in the rain forest.

At times it is difficult to gain momentum or strength to carry on when others do not support your goals. They may tell you it cannot be done and you are wasting your time, but in the end you are the one who decides. It is nice to be surrounded by those who share your vision and believe in you. If you currently have supportive friends and family members in your corner, then this is great. But they too ultimately cannot control what happens.

Imagine you are an aspiring actor and you pack up and move to California. This means leaving your family, friends, and everyone else you know. Automatically you are in a state of distress as you face loneliness. Once you arrive in Los Angeles you are faced with a sea of obstacles. The glamour and bright lights of stardom begin to dim because the last 20 auditions you had were unsuccessful.

Casting directors can tell you everyday of the week you are terrible. But in the end you can either reject or accept it.

How fair is it to give up on a dream just because someone tells you to. Who gives them the right to make decisions for you? When someone tells me I cannot do something, I use it as fuel and add it to my internal fire that will drive me to success. I eat it up.

In fact I prefer someone tell me I cannot do it because it only makes me hungrier to achieve that goal. This is my internal process and it is ultimately my choice to succeed. You have the ability to do the same thing. Once you have decided that you want to make changes in your life, you need to follow through. Thomas Edison once said, "Our greatest weakness lies in giving up. The most certain way to succeed is to always try, just one more time." In the following chapter you will learn my story and what steps I took to reach my goals.

CHAPTER OVERVIEW

- Success or failure originates in you.
- Avoid blaming others.
- Never give up.
- Don't make excuses or wait for something good to happen.

CHAPTER THREE

MY STORY OF OVERCOMING OBSTACLES

"Our lives are not totally random. We make commitments, we cause things to happen." - Wendy Wasserstein

My roots are in beautiful Greenville, South Carolina. I was born and raised there and I have many fond memories of living in the South. Whether it was coming home to my mother's delicious southern cooking, catching lightning bugs in the evening, or taking family trips to Myrtle Beach, I always had a great time.

However, after graduating high school I found that I wasn't having so much fun. I felt lost, scared, and had no clue what I wanted to do in life. Several of my classmates went off to four-year colleges and universities while others went directly into the work force. A friend of mine, who today is a successful businessman, was in the same position as I. Throughout school we were not studious and at best resembled Beavis and Butthead. Actually, when the show aired on Music Television for the first time we thought the creators wrote it with us in mind. We were just living for the moment without direction or any planning for the future.

Shortly after graduating high school I enrolled at the local community college, not because I was committed to academia but for a much greater purpose -- meeting girls. I took a few basic courses and before I knew it I was failing most of them.

The next summer I registered for two courses at a small university near Myrtle Beach. The school accepted me on probation because of my history of poor grades in high school, low SAT scores, and even worse grades at the local community college. At the time my admission seemed like the break I was looking for and I was extremely excited. I had a schedule all planned out even before classes started. I would attend class for a few hours a day, surf in the evening, and party at night. By the end of the summer I was very tan from surfing, attended 20 or so parties, and only passed one class.

Needless to say, my plan failed and the school notified me I would not be allowed to enroll in the fall. I was crushed because I was headed back to my hometown feeling like more of a failure. Then after a year or so I began to do a little soul searching while living on a sailboat.

In the early 1990s my father owned a 33-foot sailboat named "Lucky Strike" which was kept in a marina in Daytona Beach, Florida. She was almost 20 years old but was extremely fun and easy to sail. I actually enjoyed it so much I lived on the boat for several months during the summer. As a live-aboard I saw many people from all walks of life drift in and out of the marina, from multi-millionaires to retired couples living on a shoestring budget.

On any given day there were several mega yachts in the

marina. Many of them were close to 80 feet in length with beautiful sleek lines. Every time I walked past I thought, Wow, I wonder if I will ever be successful. This caused me to really look at my life and ask what I needed to do to change things because I was very unhappy. Up to that point my only accomplishment was barely graduating high school. I didn't know exactly what I wanted to do or how I was going to do it but I knew I had to choose a different path. At that point I was committed to change.

Lucky Strike in the Halifax Harbor Marina, Daytona Beach, Florida.

My next decision was to return to Greenville, South Carolina and make another attempt enrolling at the local community college. One of the first classes I took was a basic psychology course. I struggled at first but as time went on I began to take a real interest in the material. On the first test I believe I scored a D, which was par for the course. However, I knew I could do better and I needed to show it. To better prepare for the next exam, I sought the professor's help and prepared for several days in advance. On the day of the test I felt confident and I whipped through it without a problem.

The next class, during which the test was to be returned, I arrived late. As I walked in the professor immediately asked if I could tell the class what I did. At that point I had no clue what she was talking about. I just looked at her like a deer caught in headlights. The first thought that came to mind was that I was in trouble. Then she repeated the question as everyone in the class glared at me, "Tim, could you please tell us how you improved your grade on the second exam because you made an A."

Well, I almost passed out and I wanted to ask if she graded it correctly. But before I was able to respond another student interrupted. She was an elegant young lady who was very upset. She let everyone know she had been a straight A student in high school and could not earn an A in this class to save her life. Inside I was laughing because I never made the honor roll and had only seen a few A's in my life, thanks to classes like P.E. and home economics. I told the class that I simply followed the professor's advice and that was it. I remember feeling extremely happy and I knew I could excel in academics, especially in psychology. From that moment on psychology became my passion.

After a year of improving my grades I began to plan for my next step, which was to look for a four-year university. My first choice was a small school in St. Augustine, Florida. I made a visit, toured the campus and immediately fell in love with the campus and the town.

However, the school did not feel the same about me and I was denied admission. Needless to say I was devastated. At this point I was ready to throw in the towel and I started second guessing my abilities again. I asked myself over and over, what else I needed to do to prove myself?

I was also assailed with thoughts; <u>What if I am not smart enough, what if I'm just not cut out to do well in school, maybe I should just quit and not waste anymore time in school.</u>

However, I switched my thinking around and began making more positive self-statements such as, "I will find another school, I am committed and I will succeed, I am smart enough to get into a good school, and I will prevail." I was determined to be persistent and never give up. I was on a roll and no one was going to keep me from earning my bachelor's degree. After catching my breath and regaining my composure, I began researching other educational institutions and I found Francis Marion University located in Florence, South Carolina.

Francis Marion University is a beautiful southern school surrounded by fields of billowy cotton and large trees draped with moss. Maybe the stunning campus inspired me because this time I took full advantage of my opportunity. Immediately I signed up for a full caseload of courses and I began volunteering at a local community day program for adults with serious and persistent mental illness. As time passed I studied hard and experienced a great deal of joy volunteering. My passion for psychology and purpose for improving the quality of life for others propelled me to succeed. After a year and a half of doing well, I transferred to Rutgers, The State University of New Jersey to challenge myself even more.

At Rutgers I followed my plan by joining the psychology club and Psi Chi national honor society, participated in research, volunteered at another day treatment program for the mentally ill and did everything I could to excel. After two years of hard work I experienced my biggest accomplishment in life by making the dean's list and finally graduating with honors. This was an enormous achievement as I went from the back of my high school class to receiving honors from Rutgers.

At that point I was extremely confident and I felt I could achieve anything including gaining admission into a doctoral program. However, disappointment soon found me again as my initial attempt to get into graduate school was unsuccessful. The pain of rejection was difficult and as I had done so many times before, I began to question my abilities. My negative thoughts consumed me and my self-esteem went down the tubes.

I took time to evaluate other career options by bouncing around in various jobs over the next few years. I worked as a case manager, a loading dock worker, a boat yard assistant, and a paralegal.

I was not happy. Giving up and failing was not what I wanted to do. I changed my negative thoughts to positive and made another attempt at applying to doctoral programs. Then my lucky break came and I was accepted at the California School of Professional Psychology, Fresno. Five years later I graduated with a doctoral degree in clinical psychology with an emphasis in organizational behavior. The rest is history.

If you look at the admission criteria to most colleges and universities, you will see they rely heavily on past accomplishments to predict future success. Any high school graduate with a history of straight A's, leadership positions in student government, advanced classes, participation in extracurricular activities, and high scores on standardized tests will get the red carpet treatment at many prestigious undergraduate institutions throughout the country.

However, should you have deficiencies in one or more of these areas your chance of acceptance lessens. In my case I had less than a handful of A's, no leadership positions in student government or anything else, zero advanced classes, no participation in extracurricular activities, and rock bottom Standardized Achievement Test (SAT) scores. I was about as far off the target as anyone could be. However, I overcame the odds simply because I made a choice to excel, I followed my passion, created a plan, relied on positive thinking, was persistent, and lived with purpose.

I did not go into great detail how I utilized these steps but I wanted to give you a basic idea how they came into play in my story. As you read further you will be given clear instruction how to utilize each step in improving your own life. I firmly believe anyone, no matter what the odds are, can choose to do whatever they set their minds to. Just remember your past does not equal your future. What you choose to do today is what matters. You have the ability to achieve any degree of personal, professional, and financial success you desire.

PART TWO

THE LIFE YOU ALWAYS WANTED

CHAPTER FOUR

STEP ONE: FOCUS ON PASSION

"Nothing great in the world has been accomplished without passion." – John Sibree

FINDING WHAT YOU LOVE

For years I drifted around without any real desire or drive to do anything. Sure, I wanted to be financially secure and have a wonderful career but I did nothing to fulfill those dreams until I found my passion for the field of psychology. After that, it was like a wild fire out of control.

Looking back on my childhood I can remember how much I greatly disliked selling candy bars for the baseball team. I simply had no desire to go door to door in my neighborhood and convince others they needed to buy chocolate. In the end my father would end up purchasing a few boxes just so I would feel better. I had no passion for selling anything and it showed. However, had I felt differently I would have figured out a way to sell a ton of candy.

Passion is one of the most important ingredients in life. You are given an endless supply so do not worry about running out. It is already on your shelf ready for you to use. The key to finding it is to do what you love. Ask yourself what really brings joy to your life? Is it working outdoors, writing, painting, buying real estate, running a company, selling products, taking care of people, cooking, riding motorcycles, sailing, writing computer programs, or competing in sports events? Many people know automatically what they enjoy but, they become bogged down with their current jobs and other demands of life and fail to follow the very activities that bring fulfillment.

Following your passion is easy to do. You just have to decide to do it. We have all heard stories of men and women who give up stressful careers to do something they really enjoy. Whether it is to work in a state park, train scuba divers in Mexico, or sail around the world working odd jobs in various ports of call. Those who take this step report living a much more satisfying and enjoyable life. Low stress, fewer people, warm weather, and no quotas made them much happier. Although I am not recommending everyone leave their jobs and head for the Caribbean, I do hope to show you how following your passion can change your life.

I'm sure you have heard the expression that one man's trash is another man's treasure. A career in banking may be miserable for one person but a life-long passion for someone else. It all depends on you. You just have to decide what drives and motivates you. To help you clarify what it is you are passionate about complete the following exercise.

PASSION EXERCISE

1. List four activities that bring you joy and excitement. This can include anything you currently do or aspire to do.

_____

_____

_____

_____

2. List four barriers that restrict you from either engaging in them as much as you like or from doing them at all.

_____

_____

_____

_____

Take the four things you identified as joyful or exciting and read them aloud. It is best to write, read, and repeat each one on a daily basis. This will ensure they become ingrained and stay fresh in your mind.

Next, look carefully at the list you developed regarding barriers. Ask yourself how these can be overcome. For example, if you are passionate about writing but find that a busy schedule is a barrier, then you need to change this. Build in your daily routine times that you will write. Become more structured and stick to a schedule. For example, while writing this book I set aside a few hours in the evening Monday thru Thursday and five hours each morning Friday, Saturday, and Sunday. This routine was automatic and anything else that came up during this time had to wait.

Many middle-aged adults think about going back to college to obtain a new degree. They may feel very passionate about a certain field of study but for one reason or another they choose not to enroll in a particular program. The best way for them to reach this goal is to first identify what barriers restrict them. Family and work responsibilities are often at the top followed by financial limitations. However, if they create anti-barriers they can overcome any obstacle. So there really is no excuse for not achieving any goal you are passionate about. See the list below as an example.

PASSION	BARRIERS	ANTI BARRIERS
Complete my bachelors degree	Time restraints due to family and work obligations.	Saturday and Sunday I will research on-line university programs from 10 AM to noon at the library.
Complete my bachelors degree	Limited financial resources	I will contact the college on Thursday at 9 AM and schedule a time to meet with financial aid services to determine available loans, grants and scholarships.

Now, pick one of your designated passions and complete the table below including barriers and anti-barriers. Please be as specific as possible when outlining your anti-barriers.

PASSION	BARRIERS	ANTI BARRIERS

Utilize this table with each one of your passions. You will be pleasantly surprised with the results. Always write down what it is that you desire followed by your perceived barriers and a plan for overcoming each. There is truly nothing you can't accomplish if you set your mind to it. This exercise will help you along the way.

Those I encounter who are not happy with their current life circumstances seem almost lifeless. They are only going through the motions to make ends meet but have no excitement or joy. You may be this person. Life does not have to be this way. Not everyone is miserable and we all have the choice to do what makes us happy. You are not chained to your career or job. If you believe you can make changes you will. However, believing you are stuck and unable to follow your passion will do just that, keep you stuck.

In the past I worked various jobs just to make ends meet. Day in and day out I showed up for work but I had no joy or excitement in what I was doing. I was there in person but my mind was somewhere else. Many times I found myself dreaming about what I would rather be doing. I did what was required of me but no more. I felt my life was about as exciting as watching ants carry food back and forth to their mound. But I never gave up on my dream to earn a doctoral degree in psychology. I knew it was my calling and I was determined to follow the path I had chosen. Although I experienced rejection at first, I did not give up. I continued to drive forward and never lost faith. I know if you do what you love, everything else will fall into place. I believe life is too short to sell out your dreams. The energy you feel from doing what you enjoy is truly incredible.

Many people search for that wonderful high in life in the form of illegal drugs. It makes them forget their worries and troubles and puts a temporary smile on their faces. However, the experience is short lived and the reality of their lives becomes worse than it was before the drugs. "Worse" may come in the form of an eviction notice for not paying rent or jail time after being arrested for possession.

People who have successfully stopped using drugs replaced the artificial high with a healthy alternative. Using a healthy addiction to propel you forward in life is what it is all about. Doing what brings you extreme joy and fulfillment will carry you as far as you can imagine.

However, without it you will certainly fall short. You have the key for unlocking your potential. You only need to use it, open the door, and follow your dreams to find true happiness.

KEEP THE FIRE BURNING

Once you dive in and swim with passion for some time you may notice that you begin to get tired. What seemed fun at first becomes routine and not as colorful as it once was. It's normal to be involved in a particular career or hobby for many years and all of sudden find your flame a little low. Does it happen to everyone? No. Can it happen? Yes. At some point you may become burned out and ready for a change. The drive you once had is now almost gone.

If this is the case you may need to explore a way to re-ignite your current passion or follow a new one.

TELLTALE SIGNS YOU ARE READY FOR CHANGE

Do you have trouble getting up for work every day? Do you have little enthusiasm for your job? Do you struggle to stay awake at meetings? Do you ever make self-statements such as, "I really don't like this job," or "I could care less about this report and meeting company standards." If so, your flame may be low. I am not inferring that we must all be full of happiness and energy in everything we do in order to live with passion.

If your current job duties are not satisfying, maybe look for another department in which to work. Possibly decide if a supervisory position would be more challenging and fulfilling. If you are in the real estate industry and sell residential property and feel burned out, maybe shift your focus. Investigate the option of selling commercial property or consider working toward a brokers license. Any of these changes may help you regain the passion you once had. Sometimes small changes can make a world of difference. Do not feel you have to change everything in your life if you are unhappy. Just reshape and modify certain areas to keep you passionate and fulfilled.

You can apply this principle to many things--spending time with your children, friends, or spouse for example. Should your traditional family night out for pizza lose its appeal, try something new. Explore other creative options to keep it fresh. If your weekly card night with your friends is no longer fun, suggest a different activity. Regardless of what you choose, make it exciting by changing your routine when needed.

You have probably heard that half of all marriages end in divorce. That's a pretty dismal figure but there are strategies for not becoming a statistic. First, it's common to lose the intensity you once had for being married. However, this does not necessarily mean it's time to move on. It may mean you are in need of a marriage tune-up.

When you buy a new car it runs fine but as the miles add up you need to do routine maintenance to keep it running.

Your marriage is the same way. Should you fail to maintain your car or your marriage you will surely find yourself stranded on the side of the road. When your marriage is smoking and backfiring pull over and evaluate the problem. Sometimes you may find that it's something fairly simple and you can do the repairs yourselves. Other times you may need an expert such as a therapist.

Regardless of the situation, take action at the first sign of trouble. Don't feel like your only option is to kick him or her to the curb. Work together and create new ways to spend the evening together. Maybe hire a babysitter at least one time a week so you can have alone time. Go on a spur-of-the-moment trip or do something you have never done. Don't wait for holidays or anniversaries to do something special. This should be occurring all year long. Come up with an activity you have never done before that will surprise your spouse. So what if he or she thinks you're crazy. The point is to do whatever you can to find that spark and keep your marriage running.

Don't get bogged down into routine, spice it up. Life should be about doing what is fun and exciting. If you choose to view life as full of pain and suffering you will discover just that. However, if you always look for the best life has to offer, that is exactly what you will find. You have the power to do whatever you set your mind to so find your passion and live life to the fullest. Below are several questions and answers to help clarify some of the concepts covered in this chapter.

QUESTIONS AND ANSWERS

Question:
I don't feel passionate about anything. I've searched far and wide but nothing really motivates me. What can I do?

Answer:
Most people can develop a list of various activities they are passionate about. Some can identify them rather quickly while others need more time. Should you have difficulty, find a quiet area and relax your body and mind. Being relaxed will often help you think more clearly.

Question:
My wife and I have been married 15 years and although I love her,

I believe it's time to end the marriage. I'm tired of arguing and I don't feel passionate about our relationship. Do you think it would be better to go our separate ways?

Answer:
There is no easy answer to your question. I find it hopeful that you still love her. Identify a few topics of argument and set up anti-barriers for each. For example, many couples argue about time and money. These can easily be utilized in this exercise. You may also need more professional assistance and a licensed therapist can be of great help.

Question:
I work in a high stress environment and I often think about leaving my job because I am burned out and no longer passionate. What should I do?

Answer:
First determine if there is anything you can do to reignite your passion in your current job. Is there another department to work in or other opportunities within your company to do something different? Are there other companies in the same field that would be exciting to work for? Should you find yourself completely burned out in that particular industry make a list of everything you are passionate about, even those things that are just hobbies. Many people create new careers from former hobbies. Just relax and be patient and the answers will come.

CHAPTER OVERVIEW

- Live life by doing what you love.
- Focusing on your passion will lead you to happiness and success.
- Create anti-barriers for living passionately.
- Re-ignite your passion as needed.
- Be aware of burnout and stagnation.
- You have the power to fulfill your dreams.

CHAPTER FIVE

STEP TWO: CREATE A PLAN

"The secret of getting ahead is getting started. The secret of getting started is breaking your complex overwhelming tasks into small manageable tasks, and then starting on the first one." – Mark Twain

The idea of planning has been kicked around so often that it has become stamped in our brains. How many times have you heard someone say, "plan your day," "plan on being here on time," "plan on staying late," "plan for your career,' "plan for your retirement," and "plan for a rainy day?" All this talk about planning can make your head spin. But, what does it mean to plan? I grew up being told to plan for everything under the sun but was never taught how to do it. Many other concepts in our society are kicked around the same way planning is.

For a while I worked with foster families who had children with maladaptive behaviors. One family in particular complained that their foster son would not clean his room and would lie and say it was neat. Upon further inquiry they reported he spent an hour in his room each day shuffling things around. During inspection they would find dirty laundry under the bed, cups, plates, and papers in the closet, and piles of books and toys on his desk. They would become furious, yell at him and tell him to go back in the room to clean up. His response was, "I did clean it."

My first question to the family was, "Did you ever show him what a clean room means to you and your husband?" They replied, "No, but he should know what clean means, everybody knows what a clean room is." However, he believed cleaning meant not having anything lying on the open floor. This is exactly what he did. He picked up everything that was lying where you walk and either threw it in the closet, under the bed, or on the desk. His definition of cleaning was very different from the family and they did not teach him what they expected and how to clean properly.

My remedy was to have the family assist him in cleaning his room each morning for a week and make a checklist of what was expected. The following visit the family proudly announced he was doing a fine job taking care of his room and they had no other concerns.

Planning is like cleaning in that not everyone knows how to do it. We have all heard the term "plan" and know about it in a general sense, but not everyone is trained in planning. Especially, when it comes to reaching your goals and dreams.

Those who own sailboats and enjoy cruising from one island to the next always plan. A lot of preparation goes into ordering food supplies and water, first aid, mapping their course, emergency equipment, boat preparation, money, legal documents, and weather forecasts. Without thorough preparation and planning sailors may not make it to their destination or survive. It takes careful planning to make a successful voyage.

Similarly, you need to pay particular attention to your plan of action. If your passion is to start your own business, you will need to develop an extensive business plan. How much money will you need for marketing, supplies, salary, merchandise, rent, utilities, insurance, attorney, and accounting fees? If you do not develop some sort of plan, you increase your chance of not succeeding. Now, let's look at six practical steps in planning that, when implemented, can help you reach any of your goals.

STEP 1-HAVE CONFIDENCE

Never sell yourself short. You have the capability and power to accomplish anything you desire. If you always wanted to be self-employed, go for it. As they say, "Shoot for the moon!" Why settle for less when you can have exactly what you want? The first step is to have confidence in your abilities. Many people do not have a close family, an exciting career, or financial security because they truly don't believe it will ever happen. If you poll 20 random people on the street and ask them if they deserve to be happy and financially secure, I'll be willing to bet all 20 will tell you yes, they deserve it all. But how many of them have this? Probably very few. If they really felt it could happen, they would be working toward creating a better life for themselves.

STEP 2-NO NEED TO RECREATE THE WHEEL

Whether you want to become involved in investing, change careers, go back to school, or improve your relationship with a loved one, chances are someone else has already been successful at making that transition. Take the time to research what others have done that made their journey successful. There are a number of self-help books detailing almost everything anyone has done. Pick one up at your local bookstore to discover the secrets. The other option is to find someone who is doing exactly what you want to do. Call them up, introduce yourself and ask questions. Most people will be happy to share their experience and even mentor you.

Sam Walton the founder of Wal-Mart made it no secret that he copied what other retailers were doing when he started his business. He was known for developing all sorts of disguises in order to enter his competitor's stores as a shopper. His plan was to investigate everything from their displays and store set up to prices. Whatever he liked he copied in his own establishment.

The trial and error method works, but you can save time by learning from others, especially from their mistakes.

The internet is another great resource for learning just about anything. It really is amazing how much information is stored there. With the click of a mouse you can have the world at your fingertips. There are also groups, message boards, and sites dedicated to helping you. This is by far one of the best resources out there.

STEP 3 – UTILIZE SMALL STEPS

Once you determine your goal and have a general idea of what steps to take, start working your plan little by little. Doing the little things always gets you further down the road. No matter what it is, take it one step at a time and don't get carried away with all the details. Too often we want to do too much too soon and become tired and/or paralyzed. Take it easy and pace yourself just as you would if you were running in a marathon.

In writing this book I did a little each day. I knew I couldn't stay up day and night for weeks on end and expect to crank it out. I would definitely burn out and do a poor job. It brings me joy when I do something each day that brings me closer to my goal. No matter how small a step you take, it is a step nonetheless.

STEP 4-DON'T WORRY ABOUT AN INCOMPLETE PLAN

Too often people do not start working toward their goal because they feel as if they don't have enough information.

Before they know it, days, months, and years go by without any progress. They still do not feel comfortable taking action because of missing details. The fact is you do not need all the pieces of the puzzle to begin putting it together. The best course of action is to gather as much information as you can and begin your journey. The rest will come and you will learn as you go. Don't worry, everything will eventually fall into place. You may make mistakes along the way but that will happen even with a well thought out plan. So don't be frozen, just start your journey as soon as possible.

When I moved to beautiful Costa Rica from California, I did not have all the answers or even know what to expect. I knew it was a step in the right direction but that was it. I wasn't guaranteed it would work out but I knew it was part of my plan.

When I first arrived here I experienced culture shock. Not only was the scenery different, there were many other factors I never imagined would affect me. For example, the language barrier was difficult, the slow pace of life was frustrating, I missed my friends, and the roads always in terrible condition. Had I known how difficult it would be I may have chosen not to take this step. But as time went by, I learned to cope with all the elements and fell in love with the country and the people who live here.

Looking back this has been one of the best experiences

in my life and I have grown as a person because of it. It just goes to show that you don't need all the answers. As obstacles come your way you will figure out how to handle them. Learn to adapt and cope with unexpected circumstances and you will be successful. In fact, it may be a blessing that you do not fully know what to expect. Too often fear sets in like a dense fog and takes over if you become overwhelmed with details. The truth is that it isn't so much about lacking the necessary information as it is about coping with fear.

STEP 5-COPE WITH FEAR

Fear of failure is the number one reason most people do not strive for their goals. Don't be afraid of failure, embrace it when it comes and use it as a method of learning. It is not the end of the world if you fail, because eventually you will reach your goal. Do not let fear control you and especially do not be afraid of what others think.

It's very sad to think that fear controls many people's lives. The fact that fear can put a wedge between you and your dreams is disheartening. Anthony Robbins described fear as an acronym for "false evidence appearing real." How many times have you anticipated an event you believed would be horrific? However, after it was over you thought, That's it? That wasn't so bad. We create a sense of fear from our fantasies, which are just that, fantasies, and not the real world.

The most effective strategy to combat fear is to create a positive mental picture of yourself achieving your goal. Having positive thoughts and creating a clear picture of success in your mind is extremely powerful. Too often we envision ourselves failing. Once this occurs we spiral into the bottomless pit of venom-laced feelings.

If my passion is to buy investment property and I focus on everything that can go wrong including losing all my money, I am going to be plagued by negative feelings and paralysis.

However, should I focus on being successful and on increasing my knowledge of investing I will experience positive feelings and I will be much better off. Holding strong to your vision of success will keep negative thoughts from appearing. Also, continually remind yourself that setbacks are not failures. They are learning experiences. One of my favorite quotes is, "Greatness is not achieved by never falling, but by rising every time we fall." - Anonymous

STEP 6–ADJUST YOUR PLAN

Should you encounter a need to change your course along the way, feel free. This is not rare and should be expected.

Just as if you were hiking to the top of a mountain and the trail was washed out, you would choose a different route. An old Chinese proverb says, "There are many paths to the top of the mountain but the view is all the same." Too often we feel like we must quit if our chosen path does not work. The key is to regroup, search for alternative paths, and take action again.

If, for instance, you desire to climb the executive ladder in your organization but find they only hire outside the company or have turned you down, continue trying. Consider other duties to add to your curriculum vitae that make you more appealing and look for senior level positions at other companies. Don't ever stop because someone or something threw a wrench in your plan. Take it in stride, shift gears, and keep on trucking.

STEP 7–KEEP YOUR GOAL IN MIND

No matter what happens stay focused on what you want. Remind yourself why you are working hard. Whether it is a verbal reminder or visual reminder, keep it handy and ready to use. Should your goal consist of having your private pilots license, find as many pictures of planes as you can. Tape them up on the fridge or post them on a memo board. Look at it everyday to keep it fresh in your mind. Next, begin writing down everything you can think of about your dream.

If your goal is to own a house in Maui, Hawaii start picturing yourself living there. Write out exactly what you think you will need to purchase it. How much money will it take for the down payment, how much will your mortgage be, what type of insurance will you need?

Maybe you aspire to become a restaurant owner in a coastal resort area. Find a building design that you like and develop several table and chair arrangements. Make a list of all the supplies you will need, the type of training you will provide for your staff, what your food order will consist of, what cleaning products will you purchase, what type of plates and glass wear will you order, and what type of people will you hire. Use this information to keep you motivated and in touch with your goal.

Too often we get bogged down in our day-to-day life and lose track of our goals. Don't let this happen to you, keep motivated and keep your goal in sight. Complete the exercise below to help you clarify several necessary steps in achieving your goal. Focus on small steps that you can begin working on today. The sample exercise below is designed to help you clarify your goal, improve planning and become aware of resources.

Example:
1. List one of your goals.
Rekindle the relationship with my wife.

2. Describe five small steps you can take immediately to achieve this goal.
Schedule the babysitter to watch the children every other Saturday night while I take my wife out. Meet my wife each

<u>Wednesday at noon for a lunch date. Send her one special gift a month. Take part in one of my wife's hobbies each weekend. Provide her with a positive comment daily such as I'm proud of you and your accomplishments at work, you look beautiful, thanks for helping me.</u>

3. What resources can you use to assist you along the way?
<u>The babysitter, reading a book on improving my marriage, thinking more positive about my marriage each day, and scheduling time each week for her.</u>

This example should help guide you in completing the exercise below. Be very specific in your goal, each step in achieving it and the resources you will use. Notice that the plan did not say go out to lunch with my wife. It specified that I would take her out each Wednesday at noon. That way I can automatically write it in my schedule each week. Try to be as specific as you can when completing the exercise.

PLANNING EXERCISE

1. List one of your goals.

___

___

2. Describe five small steps you can take immediately to achieve this goal.

___

___

___

___

3. What resources can you use to assist you along the way?

_____

_____

_____

_____

_____

By answering these questions you are committing to your desired goal. Even if you have a good idea what you want and how to get there, write it down. Writing is very powerful and it will give you the edge you need to be successful. Whether you desire to switch careers, retire early, or improve your quality of life at home you will always need a plan.

QUESTIONS AND ANSWERS

Question:
I think planning is great but it really stresses me out when I analyze everything I have to do to reach my goal. Most often I become so overwhelmed that I just quit and never follow through. How should I overcome this temptation to quit?

Answer:
That's one of the most frequent responses people have about planning. Planning is great as it sheds light on all the things that need to be done but on the flip side it can easily overwhelm you if you let it. The trick is to focus only on two things at once, the end result and the step directly in front of you. If you do this and have faith in yourself you will have a successful journey.

Question:
When planning I always worry about being too detailed because situations always change. What is the best strategy?

Answer:
You're absolutely right. Some of the steps in your plan will change. However, it's always best to be as specific as possible. Having your plan clearly outlined will get you moving. As you continue down the path you will be pleasantly surprised that many identified steps will not change. The biggest problem is that people are too vague in their planning. For instance if one of your plan steps is to visit several banks for funding your business, be clear how you will do this. For example, visit one bank on Monday at noon, one on Wednesday at 9:00 a.m. and one on Friday at 3:00 p.m. If something comes up on Monday that doesn't permit you to go, switch it to Tuesday at noon. Just reschedule and keep moving.

Question:
I know the plan steps in my head. Why do I need to write it down?

Answer:
Transferring information from your brain to paper will strengthen your plan by highlighting all the necessary details you may have not thought about. It also sets the stage for accountability. Once you write it down you are committing yourself to change. We often think about doing a lot of great things but we don't always follow through. Give yourself the best chance for success by doing everything that will give you the edge and propel you toward your goal.

CHAPTER OVERVIEW

- Utilization of a plan will increase your chances of being successful.
- Seven steps in planning include: Have confidence, follow others, take small steps daily, don't worry about missing information, cope with fear, adjust your plan as needed, and keep your goal in mind.
- Always write down your goal, plan and resources.

CHAPTER SIX

STEP THREE: THINK POSITIVE

"If one man thinks he can do a thing and another man thinks he cannot, they both are right" - Henry Ford

Alexander III was the king of Macedonia between 336-323 BCE. He became the ruler of many nations by leading his army to victory in Asia, Syria, Egypt, and Persia, all by the time he was 25 years old. He was one of the most influential kings who ever lived. But how did he accomplish such remarkable results? The answer is simple. Scholars have noted that Alexander believed wholeheartedly he was indestructible and divine. He was known as the son of gods.

Alexander's core beliefs in himself and the skills of his troops radiated so much that they followed him into battle even when enormous odds weighed against them. They continued to defeat nation after nation and grew stronger with each victory. Alexander's belief in his abilities set the stage for his incredible life.

What if Alexander had dwelled on his weaknesses and on defeat instead of victory? Would he have accomplished as much? If his troops saw defeat in his eyes would they have followed him into battle? The answer is no, absolutely not. For Alexander to succeed he needed to believe in his skills and that of his men. Those who go into battle or approach life with images and thoughts of defeat have already sealed their fate. Just as Alexander did, you must suit up each day with positive thoughts to achieve your goals and dreams.

The bottom line is that you become what you think about. If you allow thoughts of pessimism and despair to penetrate your mind, you will live a dismal life. However, if you fill your mind with positive thoughts, you will be rewarded with positive outcomes. Believing you can obtain anything you set your mind to is a very important step in becoming successful. Believing you are not worthy or skilled enough to be financially secure will certainly keep you from seeing fortune.

If you believe you are worth twenty-five thousand dollars a year, you will make exactly that. However, if you believe you are worth one million dollars a year you will find a way to earn it. It's all up to you. You just have to believe in yourself wholeheartedly.

CORE BELIEFS

Core beliefs are your internal thought processes about yourself, others, and the world. It is how you view the big picture and where you fit in. If you view the world as dangerous, unpredictable and cruel you will react accordingly. If you believe people are mean spirited, untrustworthy, and selfish you will never allow them close to you.

If you view yourself as weak, vulnerable, and unworthy

you will radiate this to those around you. Creating your world after this model will never allow you to live to your full potential. You will always look for ways to validate your predictions and to further cement your core beliefs. For example, if you view the world as dangerous and your car is stolen while at the grocery store you may say to yourself, "See, the world is cruel, people are mean spirited and I am vulnerable."

Have you ever examined your core beliefs? Many people are unaware of how they view the world, others and themselves. Take a moment to write out your beliefs. Often we want to paint our picture brighter than it really is so take a few moments before writing your answers.

EXERCISE I.

1. What are three core beliefs you have about the world?

_____

_____

2. What are three core beliefs you have about people?

_____

_____

3. What are three core beliefs you have about yourself?

_____

_____

Upon examination of your responses, were they positive, negative, or a mixture of both? Some people find they have a mixture of positive and negative. However, someone who describes the world as mostly dangerous with some enjoyable aspects is very different from someone who states the world is mostly enjoyable with a few negative factors. The person who describes the world as mostly enjoyable will live more freely and take chances in life. The other will create a wall around himself and limit his exposure to the world, thereby limiting his opportunities.

How do you view yourself? Did you list qualities such as confident, optimistic, diligent, motivated, intelligent? Perhaps you described yourself in weaker terms like unsure, cautious, pessimistic or unmotivated. Your view of yourself is one of the most important factors in becoming successful. Even if everyone around you believes in you but you doubt yourself, you will never succeed.

The upside is you can change your pattern of thinking for each of these areas. Just because you spent the last five, ten or even thirty years thinking negative about the world, others or your abilities, you can change it today! The way to rid your self of all negative beliefs and thoughts is to challenge them.

CHALLENGE NEGATIVE BELIEFS AND THOUGHTS

If you described the world as dangerous, turn it around to a more positive statement. "Yes, there are dangerous situations in life however, there are also many exciting opportunities that can bring me joy." You first acknowledge the danger then shift your focus toward the many benefits the world has to offer. Acknowledging negative thoughts and transforming them in a more positive light takes practice. However, the more you do it the easier it becomes.

Public speaking never came easy to me. I can remember many times before a class presentation I would start to sweat, have shortness of breath, and feel like my heart was literally going to jump out of my chest. I definitely struggled and at times thought I was just not cut out to speak in front of groups. My feelings of inadequacy only intensified when I watched others who appeared to talk with ease. I would create negative thoughts about my abilities, such as: <u>I'm terrible at speaking</u>. <u>Other people do it so much better than I</u>. <u>Why do I keep trying</u>? <u>What if my classmates believe I'm lousy</u>?

What I did to turn it around to become a better speaker was to challenge this thought process. Now I fill my mind with self-statements such as: There are times I will stumble but overall I am very good at what I do. It's normal to be nervous when speaking in front of a crowd but I know what I'm talking about and I will do just fine. Not everyone has to agree with what I say. I take pleasure in public speaking and that is what matters. Powerful positive statements like these will propel you to reach any goal.

Your core beliefs will dictate much of what you accomplish in life. By changing negative beliefs to positive self-statements you give yourself a solid framework upon which to build. Whether you are at work, in the home, or with the in-laws, you can choose to interpret various circumstances in a more positive light. One of the most popular complaints I hear has to do with attending family gatherings. Those who do not look forward to these functions have all sorts of negative thoughts running through their minds. They believe it will be boring, the kids will be bothersome, aunt Gracie will get drunk and embarrass herself, and uncle Bobbie will ask for money again.

If you processed your family function in this manner you would probably not show up. However, turn it around by preparing yourself to have a good time no matter how loud the children scream, no matter how drunk aunt Gracie gets, or if uncle Bobbie begs you to give him money. There are other reasons for attending that make the event more desirable. For example, your husband or wife will feel supported by your attendance, you will get to catch up on how everyone is doing, great food will be served and it's a chance to get out of the house. If you think positive thoughts you will find that you have a good time.

The same applies to work settings. We often spend more time on the job than we spend with family. Most employees are not happy with their boss, co-workers and job demands. If you are like most, the Monday morning ritual is to grunt, groan, and complain how bad you have it. How often have you heard these responses after someone is asked how they are doing? "I'm doing o.k. for a Monday." "I'm just hanging in there until the weekend." or "Thank God it's Friday." This statement even became so popular a famous restaurant chain was born, TGIF (Thank God It's Friday).

Is it written in law that we should all be miserable at work and only live for the weekends? Or do we create negative associations with the workplace? I'm sure we can all attest that Monday's are not designed for disappointment and misery. When I go on vacation and it happens to be Monday, I feel fine. No problems whatsoever. I'm as happy as can be. So that narrows it down to my interpretation of work.

If you think you will have a miserable time in the office, I'll be willing to bet you will have a terrible experience. If you expect that your boss and co-workers will make you upset, I guarantee you will find something to be upset about. It's all up to you how you choose to interpret your world. The following page contains more examples for transforming negative internal statements into productive thoughts.

TURNING NEGATIVE INTERNAL STATEMENTS INTO POSITIVE SELF-TALK

TABLE I.

NEGATIVE INTERNAL STATEMENTS REGARDING WORK	TRANSFORMED INTO POSITIVE SELF-TALK
Monday's are lousy	Today is the beginning of a new week and good things will happen
My coworkers are loud and annoying	My fellow employees are unique and have many good qualities
Our customers always drive me crazy	Customers have a right to expect excellence service.
No one cares what I think so I will just keep quiet	My ideas do not always have to be implemented in order for me to feel valued.

Now think of four ongoing negative internal statements you often make about your career, personal life, and financial situation. Fill out the three following charts with negative self-statements you often make and practice rephrasing each one more positively.

TABLE II.

NEGATIVE INTERNAL STATEMENTS REGARDING YOUR CAREER	TRANSFORMED INTO POSITIVE SELF-TALK

TABLE III.

NEGATIVE INTERNAL STATEMENTS REGARDING YOUR PERSONAL LIFE	TRANSFORMED INTO POSITIVE SELF-TALK

TABLE IV.

NEGATIVE INTERNAL STATEMENTS REGARDING YOUR FINANCES	TRANSFORMED INTO POSITIVE SELF-TALK

Make copies of these tables and carry them with you. Review each positive statement daily and say aloud. Then post it where it can be seen, at your desk, refrigerator, or nightstand for example. By writing, reading, and repeating each on a daily basis you will train your brain to think positive and combat negative thoughts. Use this strategy with any situation and you will be amazed at the results.

If you fill your mind with positive thoughts about your job, family life, personal skills, or future goals, you will have a better outcome. You will need to continue this exercise daily. Also, catch yourself making negative statements and swiftly cut them off.

COGNITIVE THERAPY

Cognitive therapy is very popular today among psychologists working with clients with various diagnoses. Cognitive therapy was founded in the 1960s as a result of research conducted by Aaron Beck. It has been shown to be very effective for treating many problems including depression.

I often utilized cognitive theory when working with clients. I explored their thought processes in order to better understand what negative internal statements are creating problems. Clients in emotional distress often have negative thoughts driving their emotions whether they realize it or not. For example, if a client becomes anxious each time he goes in public his belief system may be, "People are dangerous," "Someone may make fun of me," "I may trip and make a fool of myself," "Everyone will reject me," "I may do something I regret." If his thoughts are filled with these self-statements he will become anxious, have panic attacks, and stay indoors. If his core thoughts are positive he will have a different experience. For example, "I have a number of good qualities that make me special," "The world is full of new and exciting people and activities and I am going to take advantage of every moment I have on earth." Thoughts like these will propel him to be out into the world mingling with other people.

What you focus on will determine your experience. If you focus on failure, danger, and bad people, I guarantee you that is what you will find. The message here is that you must change your thinking to take your life to a higher level.

Just think what you can accomplish by changing your thoughts. You can obtain the position of CEO, make as much money as you desire, meet a loving and caring partner to spend your life with, or buy the house you deserve to live in. It's all up to you! If you believe in yourself enough you will succeed. You are the only factor holding yourself back from creating the life you want.

Think of it as putting yourself in the driver's seat of life. You have a full tank of gas and a vehicle that will get you there. Will you just sit parked in your driveway dreaming about driving it around or will you crank the engine and go? Will you focus only on crashing or being stranded on the side of the road due to engine failure? Or will you believe you will have a safe journey and no matter what happens you will cope just fine? You have the power and ability if you just believe.

Let me ask you this. Is it fair for others to have a comfortable life, financial security, and fulfilled dreams while you do not? I'm sure you were quick to answer no. You are just as special and deserving as anyone else. Do not fall into the trap of thinking you are not smart enough, educated enough, fast enough or talented enough to make your dreams come true. The truth is you do not need to be any of these to succeed. Plenty of people have more of this, that, and the other than I do. However, it does not matter because it does not place them ahead of me for achieving anything better in life. It is ultimately up to me to make a better life for myself. This also applies to you because you also have the same opportunities as anyone else. You just have to believe.

THE POWER OF VISUALIZATION

Take a moment and imagine the type of life you want to live. Can you see it clearly? What are your relationships like? Is there an abundance of joy and respect? Are you living in a comfortable apartment or a large mansion overlooking the water? How much money do you have in your bank account? What are you doing with your money? Are you able to buy your family items they need and deserve?

Will you start a non-profit organization? Will you donate money or time to a charitable cause? How will you feel when others thank you for your assistance?

What type of career are you involved in? Do you imagine waking up happy for work each day? Are you filled with excitement by accomplishing your goals?

Now let's go further and utilize visual imagery to help make your dreams real. Let's bring them to life and experience what it's like. Visualization is one of the best ways to combat fear and uncertainty. If you imagine yourself doing or having something you always dreamed of, you are making that experience familiar.

Think of it like flying for the first time. Before you ever boarded an airplane I'm sure you had all sorts of negative thoughts. The two most common are "What if the plane crashes?" "What if I get sick?" After flying several times you become more comfortable and have fewer negative thoughts. This is due to repeated positive experiences. Flying across the country becomes more familiar to you and becomes something you just do.

Visualization works on this same principle. It helps you become more comfortable by giving you the experience you need. Many top athletes utilize visualization before competing. They see themselves jumping the right distance, catching the ball in the end zone, making the three-point shot, or crossing the finish line first. They walk themselves through the steps needed to make achieving their goal familiar.

In utilizing this technique, find a quiet area away from family, friends, radio, television or anything else that can disturb you. Begin picturing yourself doing or having what you desire. Imagine every little detail and involve as many of your senses as possible. How does it look, feel, sound, smell, taste? Walk yourself through this exercise each day making your goal more familiar to you. This will train your mind and keep you focused on your goal.

QUESTIONS AND ANSWERS:

Question:
After about a week of thinking positive I start to doubt myself again. What can I do to combat this?

Answer:
Thinking positive takes continued practice. It's easy to do it once but as time goes on you may slip into your old thought patterns. This is normal and you just need to utilize your coping skills. Writing, posting, and reading your positive statements daily will help you. As in learning any new skill you have to practice.

Question:
Is there anything I can do to improve my self-esteem because I really struggle trying to think positive?

Answer:
Yes, make a list of everything you have accomplished as far back as you can remember. Make it an exhaustive list and then read it aloud over and over. Use this as inspiration that you have made progress in your life and you will continue to do so.

Question:
My wife thinks placing post-it notes all over the house with positive statements on them is ridiculous. What can I do to help her

better understand what I'm doing?

Answer:
Explain to your wife exactly what you are doing, why, and how it will benefit you. Also, try to teach her this skill and rely on each other for motivation.
Question:
I'm having a hard time using the technique of visualization. Can you provide me with a few pointers?

Answer:
The process of visualization can feel awkward at first. It's important to find a quiet setting with no one around. Close your eyes and picture yourself in that activity. For example, if your goal is to improve your presentation skills at company trainings, imagine all aspects. How is it set up, where are you standing, and who is in attendance. What are you wearing, what visual aids are you using, and what is your message. Imagine yourself being calm, confident and successful. Include as much information as possible. The more you do this the more your brain is trained to interpret presentations as fun and enjoyable, not threatening.

CHAPTER OVERVIEW

- Fill your mind with positive thoughts to benefit from the sweetness of success.

- Explore your core beliefs about the world, others and yourself.

- Your thoughts about yourself are far more important than what others think.

- Challenge negative beliefs and thoughts. Pull them from your mind and plant seeds of positive thought.

- Practice making positive statements daily.
- You will achieve any amount of success if you believe.
- Utilize the power of visualization.

CHAPTER SEVEN

STEP FOUR: BE PERSISTENT

"Continuous effort-not strength or intelligence-is the key to unlocking our potential." – Winston Churchill

Jimmy Buffett is one of the greatest musical talents of all time. He began his career in the 1970s and continues to have a strong following today. His brand of music is like none other, with songs about his adventures and love for sailing, surfing, and the sea. His concerts sell out within minutes because his loyal "parrot head" fans enjoy the atmosphere of fun and freedom. Just to have a few hours to act like a kid, sing, and dance without the hassle of real world burdens is the allure. If you take the best of Mardi Gras and mix it with a tropical paradise you'll create a Jimmy Buffett concert experience.

However, at the beginning of his career he was turned

down several times before landing a recording contract. If it were not for his persistence he would have never reached his current level of fame. He could have given up and considered work in another industry. However, he believed in himself and his music so much that he stayed focused no matter what others thought. Just remember that others may not see your dreams as clearly or as important as you do. It's up to you to continue on your quest without a thought of quitting.

EXPECTING SETBACKS

On your journey you should expect that not everything will unfold as smoothly as planned. Roadblocks and pitfalls come in many forms but they should not be a reason for you to quit, it is just the nature of the beast.

I purchased my property in Costa Rica with the idea I would subdivide the land and build three homes. Two of the homes would be sold for profit and I would live in the third one. However, before I could file the paperwork, a new law passed restricting any further subdividing.

I was upset and I complained to the architect that he did not file the paperwork fast enough. However, blaming him was not going to make my situation any better. I immediately shifted my focus from the problem toward a solution.

I sought professional advice from real estate experts in the area. They all informed me I could either build one house or sell the property. An appraisal of the land helped me make my decision to sell. Several months later I sold the land for a nice profit.

In the end I made the money I was looking for. It just wasn't how I originally planned. My setback was offset because I was persistent in finding an answer.

If you look back at your life and examine your successes you will find that persistence was a common denominator.

Your failures were only your decision to stop trying. Many

of us want to blame external factors for our defeat. The fact is that no matter how difficult it is on your journey, you are in control of how you want to react. You should always be prepared for setbacks and make adjustments accordingly and you will surely succeed.

Babe Ruth held the record for homeruns but he also struck out a lot. He once stated, "Every strike brings me closer to the next homerun." So every time you do not succeed, process it as one-step closer to your goal and not as one-step back. Remember this quote when you become frustrated with lack of progress, "Failure is, in a sense, the highway to success."
– John Keats

IMMEDIATE GRATIFICATION AND QUITTING

Many times we quit because our expectation of how soon our goal will be accomplished is not met. At that point we say, "Forget it, I'll just move onto something else." It happens all the time in everything we do. I was at the bank the other day when after five minutes I left without cashing my check because I was not helped fast enough. Had I waited, I would have accomplished my goal.

Impatience is a driving force in our daily life, whether it comes while sitting in traffic, being placed on hold while on the telephone, or waiting in line. We then adopt and transfer our impatience to long-term goals and dreams. It's a matter of not being able to delay gratification.

Everything in life these days is set up to happen fast. Think microwave dinners, drive-through food establishments, and cell phones. While driving down the interstate I once saw a young lady talking on her cell phone, applying makeup, and eating, all while she was driving. Our society is so fast paced that we don't want to wait for anything. The big problem comes when people attempt to apply their fast paced instant gratification filled lives to long-term goals and dreams.

Think about society's fixation on losing weight fast, whether it's a special pill that turns fat to muscle overnight or an operation that sucks all those cheeseburgers from around your waist. Old fashioned exercise and sweat has lost its glamour to new improved methods of weight loss. If it isn't fast, we don't want it. When we don't lose weight on a new diet we shift gears and look for another quick-fix solution. It's almost as if we are all big children who can't delay gratification. As I'm sure you know, children demand immediate results or they lose interest.

When you work with kids to improve their behavior, grades, or some other skills, you have to provide a reinforcer immediately for a job well done. This could include an hour to play video games, verbal reinforcement, or a half-hour of telephone time. However, if you set a schedule of reinforcement that is contingent on one month of successful studying before receiving an award, you will find that it doesn't work. Children just cannot delay gratification for that length of time. Children do not respond to delayed reinforcers as much as they do with immediate reinforcement. Actually, adults don't do well with delayed reinforcers either. That is why we struggle with being persistent when working toward a goal. However, there are ways to set up a system whereby you reinforce yourself daily for small steps taken toward your long-term goal.

REINFORCERS AND YOUR GOALS

Should you desire to earn your MBA, which may take at least two years, you will want to set up a system of immediate reinforcement. Otherwise, you have to wait for years to receive the reinforcer, the degree. Once you identify your steps for obtaining that goal, give yourself something special each time you accomplish a step. For example, when you study you earn the privilege of doing something fun. Utilize any activity that you enjoy. Also, after exams or major assignments, treat yourself to a night on the town such as dinner at your favorite restaurant or tickets for a show. Setting up a system whereby you reward yourself each step of the way will carry you far. Each stride you make in your plan, provide yourself something special in return. See the table below for examples of how to set up a self-reinforcement system for writing a book.

TABLE I. A SCHEDULE OF REINFORCEMENT

GOAL: Completion of Book

SCHEDULE	REWARD
Monday - 5pm-7pm Research in the library	Dinner at a restaurant of my choice
Tuesday - 12PM – 5PM Write Chapter One	Rent a movie
Wednesday – 5PM – 9PM Write Chapter One	Half-hour of internet use
Thursday – 12PM – 2PM Edit Chapter One	Purchase a new book or magazine
Friday – 8AM – 1PM Edit Chapter One and begin Chapter two	Spend three hours in a fun activity with family
Saturday – 8AM – 1PM Write Chapter Two	Take a trip to the mountains with family and friends
Sunday – 8AM – 1PM Write Chapter Two	Eat lunch in the restaurant of my choice and spend time with family

The above schedule is for one week. Each week you will need to develop a new schedule of reinforcement. This way you know what is expected in working toward your goal and what reward you will earn. Build a schedule that is specific to what you will be doing, when, and for how long. Be as specific as possible and you will be successful. If you build each component into your schedule you will find that things get done. It becomes automatic and you eliminate other competing forces such as watching television, talking on the phone, or surfing the internet.

While completing my doctoral dissertation I often found myself doing anything and everything other than what I needed to do. My house was the cleanest it had ever been because I would rather fold laundry, sweep, mop, wipe down the counters, and even clean toilets rather than run data, read articles, or write my results section.

However, before writing this book I developed an estimated time for completion and a weekly schedule to get me there. This has proved to be very beneficial because at this moment I am approximately two weeks ahead of schedule. Without being disciplined and sticking to this routine I would not be this far ahead.

You too can achieve the same results by utilizing this technique. Complete the following table for one of your goals along with reinforcers for each. Remember to utilize a reinforcement system that is immediate. Then create a fresh schedule each week with new goals along with new irresistible reinforcers. If you build this into your schedule each week it becomes automatic.

TABLE II. YOUR SCHEDULE OF REINFORCEMENT

GOAL: _____

SCHEDULE	REWARD
Monday	
Tuesday	
Wednesday	
Thursday	
Friday	
Saturday	
Sunday	

Once you have completed the table begin to implement it. Jump right in and watch your dreams begin to take shape.

It really is just a matter of keeping yourself going. This is one of the best tricks to ensure you stay on track.

THE CONSEQUENCE OF NOT BEING PERSISTENT

Often focusing not on what you have to gain but what you will lose can be just as motivating. If your goal was to become a commercial pilot and I asked you to write down every benefit of becoming one, I'm sure you would have a list a mile long. That would be very easy. However, if I asked you to write down the consequences of not taking action toward this goal you might have to think awhile. In a general sense you would be able to easily describe a few consequences but I would encourage you to dive deep and explore each of these.

Focusing on what will occur should you not achieve your goal will act as a back up if the benefits do not motivate you enough. Think of it as the double-sided door of motivation. Review the table on the following page for an example of this concept.

TABLE III. DOUBLE-SIDED DOOR OF MOTIVATION

GOAL: Owning Your Own Business

BENEFITS OF OBTAINING YOUR GOAL	CONSEQUENCES OF NOT STRIVING FOR YOUR GOAL
Feeling free and alive by following my dream	Feeling restricted and frustrated by working at the same old job
Having the opportunity for financial security	Living from paycheck to paycheck and not being able to provide for my family
Being able to compete with other businesses in a multi-million dollar market	Competing with fellow co-workers for a dollar raise.
Having control over my destiny	Having to settle for less than I deserve
Creating a company that can give back to the community in volunteer hours and funding.	Not having the opportunity to help others because I can barely help myself.

Now develop your own table with your goal in mind. Take some time to really think about this exercise because I'm sure once you are finished, you will be really motivated.

TABLE IV. DOUBLE-SIDED DOOR OF MOTIVATION

Goal: _____

BENEFITS OF OBTAINING YOUR GOAL	CONSEQUENCES OF NOT STRIVING FOR YOUR GOAL

The other day I was talking with someone about my book and the strategy I have for publishing and marketing it. He asked, "So how much will all this cost you?" I replied with an estimated figure of money and time. "Man, that seems like a pretty big risk, what happens if it doesn't work out?" he asked. At that moment I knew what was driving his comment. His thought process was such that he didn't believe he could ever write a book or feel confident enough to invest his money or time.

"Well, I don't look at it that way, I said. I focus more on what I have to lose if I don't do this. I'll be stuck in a job I'm no longer passionate about, feel miserable and stagnated for years to come and I won't have the opportunity to speak, write, or help others on a much larger scale." "Yeah, he said. I know what you mean about doing something you no longer enjoy because I feel the same way." I could see at that moment he finally understood what I was doing and why I needed to do it at any cost.

QUESTIONS AND ANSWERS

Question:
I'm not so sure I buy into all this talk about reinforcers. Can you clarify this concept?

Answer:
Reinforcement can be used in just about every area of your life. Animals and people respond well to a reinforcement schedule. This is a powerful way to shape and create new behavior. Watch any animal trainer and you will see them provide a treat for a desired behavior. This is the same process you provide yourself with each step you take toward your goal. It's so powerful you can even shape the behavior of others without them knowing it. As a graduate student I actually trained my professor to focus on me approximately 90% of the time while he lectured. In a class of about 30 students

I did this by nodding and leaning forward (the reinforcer) each time he looked at me. I did this consistently for about two weeks and shaped his behavior without his knowledge. My friends were amazed and had a good laugh. This goes to show the power of reinforcement.

Question:
I set up a system of reinforcement but it just doesn't seem to work. What can I do?

Answer:
Make a list of everything that is reinforcing to you. Include types of food, hobbies, favorite outings, vacations, or anything else you enjoy. Utilize smaller rewards for daily accomplishments and larger reinforcers for completing your overall goal. Remember they need to be frequent and powerful.

CHAPTER OVERVIEW

- Follow your dream and disregard skepticism from others.
- Expect setbacks and work through them.
- Set up an immediate schedule of reinforcement.
- Evaluate the consequences of not following your dreams.

CHAPTER EIGHT

STEP FIVE: LIVE WITH PURPOSE

"Success is not just money in the bank but a contented heart and peace of mind." – Sarah Ban Breathnach

How many times have you read articles or watched the news on the rise and fall of famous athletes, musicians, actors, or corporate leaders? They seemed to have had it all from million dollar salaries to large mansions, yachts, and a huge fan base. Yet, it ended in disaster, whether via drugs, personal scandal, corporate corruption, or suicide.

It seems clear that material possessions will not shelter you from problems in life. They will not bring everlasting joy when you are depressed. They will not bring peace of mind when you are troubled. And they will not bring meaning to life. The only way to obtain true happiness, peace, and meaning is to live your life on purpose. Expensive homes, fancy clothes, fine jewelry, and fast cars mean nothing without purpose. These are tangible items that come and go. Having them will not sustain happiness.

CREDIT CARD THERAPY

Today credit card use is the most popular way to shop. With easy access to thousands of dollars of credit, people buy items they believe will make them happy. I remember going on shopping sprees when things were not going well. One moment I was feeling down and the next I was happy after a new electronic device grabbed my attention. At the time it seemed like the perfect fix but before I knew it I was feeling sad again. This only worsened when the credit card bill arrived.

Everything from big screen televisions to food is bought on credit. After your cards are maxed out, you are left paying much more than the items are worth because of high interest rates. Not making payments on time or failing to make payments will quickly increase your rates and create a sense of desperation. You find yourself in a deep hole with no easy escape. The joy and excitement of having the newest "toys" lose their appeal very quickly. In the end these shopping sprees turn out to be anything but exciting.

When we die we cannot take anything with us. So why put so much energy into having the biggest, fastest, and best items? We do it because, first, they are fun and, second, they are available, but if all we have are material possessions without purpose in life we will not be any happier.

Do not make your personal possessions your world make your purpose the center of your universe. Purpose can be defined in many ways and can be different for every person. Living with purpose is deeper than anything you physically do; it is the meaning behind your actions. Purpose is different from passion. Your passion may be to become a surgeon or start a non-profit organization, while your purpose may be to improve the quality of life for those you serve. Passion is important and necessary for success, but it is very different from purpose. So at this point you may be wondering how do you find your purpose in life.

FINDING YOUR PURPOSE

Many look toward religion for direction. It provides guidance and a set of standards by which to live. Your purpose would be to serve a higher power and to help others in need.

Giving back to the community and helping those around you can provide a wonderful feeling that is almost indescribable. For example, volunteering at the animal shelter or a soup kitchen are excellent ways to give back to the community. The feeling you get in return is more valuable than any monetary payment.

I was able to touch the lives of many people in my first experience as a volunteer at a day treatment program for adults. I felt extremely nervous on my first day because I didn't know what was expected of me and I had never worked with anyone in the mental health system before. On my first day the director introduced everyone and put me in charge of leading recreational activities with the clients. This involved organizing board games, making arts and crafts, and engaging in outdoor activities like basketball, baseball, and kickball. The idea was to provide structured activities in which the clients could improve their interpersonal and social skills.

Each week the clients and staff seemed to appreciate my enthusiasm and caring style. The clients especially loved having a fresh set of ears to listen to their stories, many of which were very sad, but inspiring. To hear their struggles and life experiences made me humble and thankful for what I had. I was somehow able to connect with them and I truly felt their pain. They were able to sense my connection and probably trusted me because of it.

Before I knew it, I was developing groups and various other activities on my own. I even taught driver's education to some of the higher functioning adults. The goal was to help the clients develop a sense of autonomy and empowerment, and what better way to feel empowered than to have your driver's permit or license.

After several months I received volunteer of the month and then volunteer of the year awards. I never expected anything in return for my services, I just enjoyed being there. I focused only on giving and nothing else. The return for this investment was amazing. The smiles, laughs and thanks I received from the clients brought me joy and purpose in life.

Up to that point, no salary had ever brought me as much enjoyment. Here I was working for absolutely nothing--zero money--and I loved it. From that moment on my purpose in life has been to improve the quality of life for as many people as possible. It seems when I focus on giving and helping others the returns are high. However, when I focus on what I am owed, I either never receive it, or it does not carry the sensational feeling I expected. Just focusing on giving and doing the best I can in whatever I set out to do has paid tremendous dividends in my life.

WHEN YOUR PURPOSE FINDS YOU

A friend of mine and his wife went through a terrible experience. At approximately seven and a half months into her pregnancy she lost the baby. Both were devastated. They had never experienced this degree of pain. My friend told me several days later that he was mad at God and questioned his reason for allowing such a cruel thing to happen.

During our conversation he mentioned how grateful he was for all the support and help provided by family, friends and even strangers. He recalled how another couple who had experienced a similar loss reached out to him and his wife. Their kindness and blessings meant so much to my friend and his wife when they felt so alone. He stated, "I am now part of a club I never wanted to be a part of, but I really want to help others who experience the same."

I said that it seemed he had found his purpose in life. Before he was only dedicated to his business and was engrossed with making money. He always thought about money, talked about it, and wanted to hear what others had to say about it. His preoccupation with money, he believed, was his purpose, but he was not happy.

I truly believe things happen for a reason in life whether we immediately see it or not. For my friend, I think he is more humble and will be happier in the long run as he follows his newly found purpose.

LIVING WITH PURPOSE

Regardless of what your purpose is, your creativity and giving is all that matters. No matter if you help one person or a hundred thousand people, you are giving back just the same. Whether you strive to protect the rainforests or the Manatees in Florida you are living with purpose. It is what you give in life and not what you take that matters. Below is a set of questions to assist you in thinking about your purpose.

1. What are your core beliefs about the purpose of life?

_____

_____

_____

2. How will you follow your purpose?

___

___

___

3. How will others benefit by you living on purpose?

___

___

___

Once you find your purpose, everything will begin to fall into place. However, you will have to work hard to stay on purpose.

Many years ago I began taking flying lessons. One of the first skills I learned is that you have to make ongoing adjustments to fly on a direct heading. The forces of lift, thrust, weight, and drag are always acting on the airplane. Just as in life there are always forces surrounding us that require constant adjustments. If we do not make these adjustments we soon find ourselves off course.

LIVING WITH PURPOSE TAKES PRACTICE

It is normal to feel elated and purposeful one day and find that your purpose gets lost in the next. It happens to all of us. Just like learning a new skill such as riding a bicycle, driving a car, sailing, or piloting a plane you will need to learn the basics, practice and deal with problems. As time goes on you will become accustomed to your new skill of living with purpose and it will come second nature.

Life will always throw you curve balls and you must learn how to react. Will it be easy at times? Yes. Will it be difficult at times? Yes. Will you ever want to kick all this purposeful living stuff to the streets and give up? Yes. Anyone who says otherwise is just not being honest. It is part of being human. In fact, each of the five steps detailed throughout this book requires practice. Some of it will come easy but it will need continuous effort on your part to keep it going.

Before I bought my first house I knew very little about lawn maintenance and plant care. When I moved in I had a beautiful lush green lawn with wonderful plants and shrubs. I really wanted to keep them looking great, and I did what I could to maintain them. However, after several months the lawn turned brown and the flowers died.

I really had no idea what I was doing so I started to educate myself by reading and asking questions. Before I knew it my lawn was green again and the flowers were blooming. I finally figured out when to fertilize and how much to water.

As time went on I became busy with work and I let the lawn go. Then again I was faced with a brown lawn and dead flowers. The problem now had nothing to do with lack of knowledge on yard maintenance, the problem was I lacked continuous effort. I allowed other interests to divert me from attending to it and it showed. Just like keeping your yard in tip-top shape, you have to attend to your purpose and not get lazy. Stay up with your purpose and do something to renew it and keep it fresh, otherwise you may get off track.

QUESTIONS AND ANSWERS

Question:
Do I need to join a religious congregation to live on purpose?

Answer:
Joining a bible based church helps to reconnect with God and the

practice of giving. Whether you help people, animals or the planet you are living with purpose and serving a higher power.

Question:
My life is very busy and I have a difficult time finding time to give back to the community other than small donations. What can I do to give back in a much larger way?

Answer:
It's very easy to get caught up with demands of work, family and friends. However, it's not the amount or size of your assistance that matters. What matters most is that you live on purpose daily and when a situation arises for you to help, you are ready.

Should you want to donate money or time in a greater degree, try writing out exactly what you would like to do. Develop a list of five small steps to help you accomplish this and what resources you will need along the way (see chapter five, planning exercise).
For example, should you want to help a no-kill animal shelter in your town, write out five small steps for doing this. Pull out your day planner and schedule a half-hour to call and talk with them about their needs. Decide how you will raise funds. Schedule another half-hour to speak with management at your company about a fundraiser. Speak with family and fellow employees for support. Send a letter to the local newspaper for coverage. If you sit around and tell yourself you just don't have time, you certainly will never find it. Utilize others to share in the work and if you schedule each step into your daily routine you will meet with success.

Question:
Is there a minimum requirement of how much or how often you should give to live on purpose?

Answer:
Absolutely not, you decide what is right for you. However, it's very

easy to live on purpose each and every day. It could be something as simple as giving a compliment or letting the person behind you in line at the grocery counter go first.

Chapter Overview

- Material possessions without purpose will not make you happy.
- To reap real rewards in life find your purpose.
- Helping others helps you.
- Staying on purpose requires continuous effort.

PART THREE

Powerful Outcomes

CHAPTER NINE

A Picture of a Successful Journey

"The future depends on what we do in the present."
- Mahatma Gandhi

Striving for your goals personally, professionally, and financially can take a lot of work, but the rewards are incredible. Just remember it takes a lot of effort and strength to carry on when you are worn down. I have experienced my own share of setbacks in each area and continue to work hard each day. However, my own struggles often seem minimal compared to the stories my grandfather, Walter Laskis, shared with me as a child about growing up during the depression.

Walter's parents were immigrants to Chicago from Lithuania and were struggling not only to keep a roof over their heads but food on the table. Before the age of 10, he was in the busy streets doing anything possible to help the family. He told of having to fight the local bullies and even stealing potatoes from a train each time it came through town. It was a matter of survival and he was a survivor.

As a young adult, he married and moved to Miami, Florida before settling in South Carolina. From nothing he started an automotive repair shop and provided very well for my grandmother and their six children. My grandparents were married for more than fifty years. When they retired they moved to Palm Coast, Florida. There, he and my grandmother lived comfortably in their final years doing what they wanted to do after accomplishing so much.

Much of what I learned from my grandfather was taught by example. He never described specifically how he accomplished so much but it was clear that he lived with passion, planned appropriately, thought highly of his abilities, was persistent, and lived with purpose.

If you follow each of the five steps you too will be successful. This is your recipe for success. Let me share with you a few more examples.

FROM EMPLOYEE TO EMPLOYER

Jim, age 52, is married with two children. He works as a salesman at a car dealership and dreams of one day owning an automotive parts company. The idea consumes him and brings joy, happiness, and excitement when he thinks or talks about it. His passion for being self-employed radiates to those around him.

Jim then begins to create a plan for reaching his goal. It's very extensive and includes both large and small steps he must take. He doesn't have all the answers but he is confident that he has enough information to begin working. He learns about running a business, and about the amount of money needed to invest in property, building, attorney fees, accounting fees, office supplies, hardware and parts.

Answers that still evade him do not disrupt his momentum. Jim knows everything will work out as he goes along. Daily, he controls his thoughts of failure because he knows thinking positive will ensure he reaches his goal successfully. Should he allow thoughts such as, "I'll never raise enough capital," "I'm just not smart enough," or "This is too strenuous for me to do," will immediately stop him in his tracks. Jim maintains his positive thinking on a daily basis. Reminding himself that he can do it and that he will figure out a way to make everything work is necessary for his success.

Being persistent also plays a huge role in reaching his dream. Jim doesn't succumb to negativity from others who say he can never be successful or he is just taking too great a risk. He knows if he does it will kill his dream. He is not afraid of failing because there is no such thing as failure to him unless he gives up. Jim knows giving up is the biggest reason people do not reach their dreams, goals, or aspirations. No one is going to give him a parts company and if he quits, his dreams are only dreams and nothing more.

Jim strengthens himself by living with purpose each and every day, from saying kind words to strangers to giving 1% of his salary to his favorite charity. He found his purpose early in life and finds comfort and strength in helping others. He knows that giving is also a way of receiving.

After several years of hard work and persistence he finally welcomes family, friends and the public to his grand opening. Now Jim is living his dream and feels incredible. He appreciates where he is and is intent on providing top quality products and service to his customers. As a result, his business grows, his bank account fattens, and his ability to reach out to help other charitable organizations increases.

Now let's look at an example of how your personal life can benefit from these same steps. Finding your personal life in peril can be one of the most difficult experiences to work through. However, the five steps can be applied just the same in turning your home life into a happy life. Take for example a husband and wife who have been married for twenty years.

FROM A SMOLDERING FIRE TO A BURNING BLAZE

Bob works as an accountant and Julie is an attorney. They have one son Brandon, who is away at college. Although Bob and Julie live in the same house, they live separate lives.

Both work ten to twelve hours a day and only talk about what happens at their respective offices. Their marriage has no excitement, no joy, and certainly no romance. At length, Julie finds their situation no longer acceptable.

Julie focuses on how much she loves Bob and determines to recreate the intensity they had when they first fell in love. She believes the act of getting married and living together for twenty years does not automatically kill romance. Julie creates a plan for getting back on track, listing all the small and large steps she needs to take. She builds into her schedule times to see Bob alone without interference from work. She plans special trips and outings and tells Bob how much she cares for him.

Julie also fills her mind with positive thoughts such as, <u>I love my husband and I am determined to rekindle our relationship. Nothing is more important than my marriage. I'm still attractive and intelligent and Bob loves me</u>. She knows creating this internal thought process will propel her toward her goal.

She is persistent and does not give up when initial difficulties come her way. Relying on her purpose in life gives her daily strength. She is dedicated to helping women who are victims of domestic violence and she volunteers once a week at a battered women's shelter. This experience is very humbling and makes her thankful for all that she has.

As months pass she finds that Bob takes notice of her effort to improve their relationship. He takes it as a signal for him to live up to his end of the marriage. As a result, Bob follows suit and begins planning romantic trips and telling her how much he loves her. Soon they find the intensity and passion they once had and live everyday thankful for each other.

FROM HELPLESS TO HELPFUL

Now consider the story of a 60 year-old gentleman wanting to change his financial status. Mark, who was nearing retirement, began looking at his finances. As suspected, he had little money saved and was not in any position to walk away from his job. He was faced with a large amount of debt and could only sustain himself for a few months without generating any income. His thoughts were, <u>What did I do wrong? How could I have not planned for retirement?</u> What now?

Mark began down this slippery slope of negativity but stopped himself. He knew the past was the past and nothing could change that. However, he could do something today to better his situation. He pondered for several weeks about his options before it came to him that he really enjoyed the real estate market. He was handy with tools and figured he could use his savings as a down payment on an older home to be used as rental property.

Mark didn't know much about being a landlord but he developed a plan for what he needed to do. He scheduled time each week to read "how to" books, looked at property and sought help from others who had done the same. Mark built this right into his schedule, which worked like clockwork.

Mark also began collecting articles on people who had become successful buying and renting property. He used these as motivation. He filled his mind with thoughts such as, <u>I can do this because I'm smart enough. Others have done it and it really isn't that difficult. It feels good to be working on creat-</u>

ing passive income for my retirement.

Mark did not allow himself to be dragged down by any negativity, including from his family who were suspect of his newly found venture. Mark followed each step in his plan and never quit even when a few homes he bid on were lost. He kept up his spirits and his momentum and never allowed the word "quit" to enter his consciousness.

After six months Mark bought his first home and filled it immediately with tenants. He worked out all the details and was able to make $100 dollars a month of passive income. As Mark's self-confidence grew he was on the prowl for a second property and on his way to financial freedom.

As years passed Mark acquired several more homes and now wanted to help low-income families find affordable housing. As a result, he built a development of quality duplexes in inner cities. Mark's goal of following his own passion matured into a greater purpose in life by helping those less fortunate. Mark was the happiest he had ever been in his entire life because not only did he have financial security but he had a purpose as well.

Success is how you define it. Each person has his own definition. No one is wrong for wanting more or less of something, it's all individually determined. If you have a difficult time finding the inspiration you need, look for someone who has done what you want to do. Find articles online, in magazines, or in books. Keep them handy and look at them daily to keep you going. You are not alone in what you desire. There are a lot of people with some of the same goals. Open your mind and let others inspire you to achieve the level of success you desire.

QUESTIONS AND ANSWERS

Question:
It's great reading success stories but sometimes I just don't think I can do it. What advice can you give?

Answer:
Just reading about the achievements of others will do nothing for you if you don't believe in yourself. You are the only person who has control over your life. First, start with small goals and work on building your self-confidence. As you become more secure in your abilities, shoot for bigger game. Eventually you will get there, so don't give up.

Question:
I often start working toward a new goal with such intensity that it seems nothing can stop me. However, about half way through my plan I lose motivation and begin procrastinating. What can I do improve my follow through process?

Answer:
I have this same problem. Many times I come up with wonderful ideas, begin working toward them and for one reason or another I lose interest. A strategy I find useful is to think through as many aspects of a new idea as I can before actually starting to work on it. This means developing a pro and con list. If the con's are more than the benefits I may opt not to do it. Also, if I decide to do it I create a tentative plan from start to finish. This strategy has helped me finish many projects including this book.

Chapter Overview

- Success takes a lot of hard work but it can be easier than you think.
- Apply the five steps for successful outcomes personally, professionally or financially.
- You are in control of the level of success you achieve.
- Look for inspiration to keep you going.

CHAPTER TEN

The Next Step

"Men are born to succeed, not to fail."
– Henry David Thoreau

For many of you, achieving personal, professional or financial success has been difficult. It's even more challenging to maintain a level of success in more than one area at once. This has certainly been the case for me throughout my life. At times my personal relationships were going strong but I was doing terrible financially. At other times I was in good shape professionally but my personal life was in shambles. It seemed I could never maintain balance. Today I continue working hard toward wide-spectrum success. The trick is not to lose focus of the big picture. Once you identify an area of your life that needs improving don't neglect the other areas. Think of it as a pie cut into different sections and each represents a percentage of your life. Your financial, personal, and professional domains all represent a slice. But each one individually does not constitute your entire pie. If you focus too intensely on any one section you may find that you have lost much more than you have gained.

Marriages often suffer when one or both parties become too focused on their careers. It may not have been consciously but several years of building a business or earning partnership in the firm has taken a toll on the marriage. It's not a price you <u>have</u> to pay for fame and glory. Many people juggle their lives successfully because they have not lost sight of the big picture.

It takes practice but it becomes easier the more experience you have. It's running around in circles that wears people down the most. Fixing one section while dropping another is not the answer. Don't live your life in a merry-go-round fashion. Maintain your friendships, marriage, work, hobbies, all at once. This is where the big plan comes in.

CREATING THE BIG PLAN

Just as you would in creating a plan for one area, create a plan that includes everything important in your life. Include your husband or wife, children, mother and father, siblings, friends, hobbies, career, finances, and purpose. Identify your goals and develop an automatic plan for maintaining health and happiness in each area. Look back at the previous chapters and utilize the strategy outlined. It's not as difficult as you might imagine. Actually, it doesn't take more energy when you identify and automatically work into your schedule what you need to do. After awhile it becomes second nature and you will be happier.

However, life isn't cured it's managed. It will always take constant effort on your part to keep things running smoothly.

Don't despair when problems arise. It's just the way things happen and you roll with the punches so to speak. You will always prevail in some way or another. At the moment a tragedy occurs it seems all is lost. However, you will pull through and you will be back on track. It's falling into the negative thinking trap that really sets you back. Look back to chapter six whenever you need a refresher how not to let negative thinking take hold. Don't throw in the towel and give up. Keep your head high and move along with whatever comes your way. At times you may become burned out and no longer able to deal effectively with life's demands. This is not the end because there are several ways to bounce back and get back on your game.

SIGNS YOU NEED A BREAK

How many times have you found yourself feeling like nothing is going right? You are mentally and physically drained and just can't take work or family pressures anymore. At some time or another we have all gotten to this point. I can remember many times waking up with a headache and dreading going to work or having to deal with family. I begin snapping at people and have little patience for anyone or anything. I'm sure some of this sounds familiar to you.

It's normal to sometimes feel overwhelmed as you try to keep pace by juggling each area of your life. After a while you become burned out and just exhausted. When this happens to me, I do something special to recharge my batteries and to gain a new perspective.

Sometimes I take a few days to just get away from it all. Putting distance between you and your daily routine can be just what the doctor ordered. I find solace in doing something different away from stress. Even just a short time away can help tremendously. The idea is to relax, let go, and regroup. Come back refreshed and ready to go. However, escaping for several days isn't always possible. For these occasions try exercise.

Going to the gym, golfing, playing tennis, surfing, and jogging are wonderful and healthy ways to regain your mental strength. I often go to the gym and work out with weights. I utilize my frustrations to help me get through those last couple of repetitions. Just when I think I can't lift the barbell one more time I remember what or who I'm frustrated at and I blast through it in a cathartic fashion. I channel my energy into my muscles and use it to build me up, not tear me down.

I also find surfing to be one of the most effective ways to recharge my batteries. Whether I'm dropping into a wave, paddling through the white water, or sitting and waiting for the next set, I'm in heaven. When I return to land I always feel refreshed and ready to take on my next task.

In Tamarindo, Costa Rica with my brother Jon Paul.

Here we are surfing the same wave. Even though they were small my brother and I had a blast.

Too often negative energy and frustration lead people to drugs, alcohol abuse, overeating, smoking, violence or other self-destructive measures. It just doesn't need to be this way. You can use this same energy for positive outcomes.

Channeling negative energy can be your biggest weapon against life's demands. Most everyone tries to manage life in some form or fashion, but choosing healthy methods will ensure you reach your goals. If you are living life to the fullest and enjoying what life has to offer, you will want to live as long as you can. Give your family, friends, and most importantly yourself the honor of being around for as long as possible. In fact, take it one step further by helping those around you reach their goals.

TEACHING OTHERS

Once you feel comfortable with the steps outlined in the book teach those around you. Help them in their journey to be successful. This can create a level of success that is very powerful. It may be that your spouse or good friend could really benefit from a better strategy in reaching goals. Once you help someone else it helps to solidify the techniques you use and boost your self-confidence. Motivate each other when times get tough. Having this buffer around you can sometimes mean the difference between goal attainment or stagnation.

When I surround myself with others who have similar goals and beliefs I seem to always rise to the occasion. However, it's easy to fall into negative habits and beliefs that others have who aren't motivated or willing to better themselves. As an undergraduate at Rutgers University, I surrounded myself with everyone who was passionate about learning and doing well in school. Their success in academia helped me to persevere when the going got tough. I didn't want to be the only one in the group to do poorly.

I had enough of a history of that. This helped me focus and buckle down when the situation arose. I know ultimately I am responsible for my success or failure and I want to give myself any advantage possible.

When I meet those who are pessimistic about life, I first try to help them see it doesn't have to be that way. If someone is unwilling to listen or is not in a position to understand, I respect that and leave them alone. I don't try to force my belief on my friends or colleagues. However, I don't allow others negativity to pull me down either. I surround myself with as much positive energy as possible.

Donald Trump made an interesting statement on his show, "The Apprentice." As you may know, two teams of candidates compete for a chance to work for Mr. Trump for a year. When a team loses a challenge he brings them into the boardroom and fires someone.

During one of these boardroom meetings, Mr. Trump told a contestant that his performance had dropped since being paired with two other members. He said something to the effect that if you hang out with losers you become a loser.

If you find that you do not have a lot of positive influence around you, go out and meet new friends. Join an organization, club, or attend a conference and network with others. Find a way to access those with similar interests, goals, and motivation. The benefits are great because not only will you learn new information for your plan, you will also be able to feed off their enthusiasm and motivation. Give yourself the edge any way you can. But, in the end, you are the most important factor in your success.

QUESTIONS AND ANSWERS

Question:
I find I don't have enough time in the day to put the same amount of energy into every area of my life. What can I do?

Answer:
Schedule, schedule and schedule some more. Build into your weekly plan everything you need to do at home, in the office and with the family. If you schedule time to spend with family, don't then type reports or read business articles. Whatever you choose to do, give 100% of yourself during that time. Too often we don't define boundaries so we become consumed with everything at once. Remember, everything in your life equals only a piece of the pie. You need balance to be truly happy.

Question:
There are times when I need a break but my professional and family obligations don't always allow it. What can I do?

Answer:
Even the busiest of people can find time for themselves. It doesn't have to include a five-day trip alone on a deserted island. Taking fifteen minutes twice a day can prove extremely helpful. Let those

you work or live with know that you will not be available at a specific time.

Turn off all cell phones, computers, beepers, radios, and TV's. Take time to exercises or go for a walk. This usually can be enough to help you regain your mental and physical strength.

Question:
I would like to teach others the skills I have learned but I'm concerned they may have questions I can't answer. What should I do?

Answer:
This is a common fear many people have when they attempt to teach a new skill or concept. However, you will never have all the answers. The best way to learn what you don't know is by teaching. When I encounter a question I can't answer I don't dance around it or pretend I have the answer. I usually respond by saying, "That's a great question, but unfortunately I don't have an answer. Let me do some research and I will get back to you." Most people will respect and trust you when you are honest.

Chapter Overview

- Don't focus too intensely on one goal while neglecting other areas of your life.
- Incorporate a plan that strives to create wealth personally, professionally, and financially all at once.
- Recognize when you are burned out.
- Utilize physical exercise to help you regroup.
- Helping others helps you.
- Surround yourself with others who bring positive energy with them.

CHAPTER ELEVEN

My Thoughts To You

"It's what you learn after you know it all that counts."
– John Wooden

Now that you have read this book, arm yourself with the strategies outlined, take charge of your life and never again settle for less. If you have followed other programs aimed at creating change and had little result, ask yourself why? Maybe the program wasn't right for you or maybe you just lost your drive. The bottom line is everyone has the capacity for change. You owe it to yourself to start the process today. Utilize the simple steps outlined throughout this book to obtain the treasures you deserve. You no longer have to walk around feeling miserable. Don't make up excuses why you can't change. And don't procrastinate.

Change can be difficult and sometimes more frightening than staying in your current circumstances. Experiencing change whether it's positive or negative can cause great discomfort. Think back to when you first left home. You were probably excited to finally be away from adult supervision and to experience freedom. However, I'm sure there was some discomfort due to the uncertainties of being alone and the reality of more responsibility. But, you did it anyway because you knew this was the next step in being an adult. Think of all your goals as being that next step you must take.

I shared with you a number of success stories throughout this book. These stories are meant to inspire you and demonstrate that incredible results can be achieved by anyone who wants it bad enough. I always enjoy reading the accomplishments of others because I generate great strength from them. Many times I leave articles around the house to remind myself of what it is I am working toward and that others have achieved. The trick is to never lose sight of what you desire. Always keep it in your mind and in your heart. This will generate an endless supply of energy to keep you going even when the going gets tough.

Life can provide you with an abundance of joy, happiness, and fortune if you allow it. Always focus on what is great in your life and everything you can do to make it better. Follow your passions and create all the wealth and fulfillment you deserve. You are unique and can accomplish anything you desire. Intelligence, luck, and even all the support in the world are not as powerful as your belief in yourself. If you believe you can climb the highest mountains in life, you will do just that. You are responsible for creating and accomplishing your biggest goals.

If you truly are passionate and see many benefits ahead, you will succeed. Never allow fear to control you because fear will stop you almost immediately. Shift your thoughts to a more positive process and work through it. Use this book as your guide in your journey. Should you need help along the way in creating positive thoughts, review chapter six, or if you need assistance in another area, refer to that chapter as well. Think of it as your own personal life coach waiting to assist you.

You have total control to choose where you go in life. Imagine yourself at the helm of a ship and you can turn the wheel to the left or right. It's your choice. If the pace is too fast, pull back on the throttle. When the fog sets in over the water, pull out your map. Identify where the danger lies and proceed with caution. Should there be a storm directly ahead, change course. Navigate around it and move on.

Even if your plan is to maintain a specific heading you can always add a new step that was initially unforeseen. Monitor your ship's equipment and current stability. Should your engines begin running hot, shut them down, fix the problem, and move on until you reach your destination.

The more experience you have at sea and in successfully navigating toward your goals, the more confident you become. <u>You will find that your success lies in focusing on solutions, not problems</u>. Once you have mastered these skills teach others how to captain their own ships and experience the joy of giving.

Make a decision right now to navigate your ship and find your Costa Rica. You can succeed and obtain all the happiness you desire. Utilizing the steps in this book can help turn your dreams into reality. Let me leave you with a quote by Henry David Thoreau. "If you have built castles in the air, your work need not be lost; that is where they should be. Now put foundations under them."

If you enjoyed this book, please feel free to visit www.lex-t.com or contact me at tim@lex-t.com. I welcome your thoughts, questions and adventures.

Index

Aaron Beck, 85
admission criteria, 46
Alexander III, 75-76
A picture of a successful journey, chapter nine, 115-121
    chapter overview, 121
    employee to employer, 116-117
    helpless to helpful, 119-120
    question and answer, 120-121
    smoldering fire to a burning blaze, 118-119
Babe Ruth, 93
being ready for change, 20-23
Bob Bitchin, 19-20
choices, 17-20
clients in treatment, 16
community college story, 43-44
coping with negativity, 32-33
defense mechanisms, 34-35
Donald Trump, 128-129
expecting setbacks, 92-93
fear, 68-69
Florence, South Carolina, 45
Francis Marion University, 45
goal exercise, 23
Greenville, South Carolina, 41, 43
Jimmy Buffett, 91-92
marina story, 42-43
my grades, 46

my story, 41-47
myths of success, 31-39
my various jobs, 46
Passion, chapter four, 51-61
    barrier exercise, 54-55
    chapter overview, 60-61
    finding what you love, 51-57
    keep the fire burning, 57
    marriage tune-up, 58
    passion exercise, 53
    question and answer, 59-60
    ready for change, 57-59
Persistence, chapter seven, 91-102
    chapter overview, 102
    consequence of inconsistency, 98-101
    double sided-door of motivation, 99-100
    expecting setbacks, 92-93
    immediate gratification, 93-94
    improving children's behavior, 94
    question and answer, 101-102
    reinforcers, 94-97
    table I, II, III, IV, 95,97,99,100
Planning, chapter five, 63-74
    acronym for fear, 68
    adjusting your plan, 69
    an incomplete plan, 67-68
    chapter overview, 74
    coping with fear, 68-69
    don't recreate the wheel, 65-66
    foster families, 64
    keeping your goal in mind, 69-72
    planning exercise, 71-72
    question and answer, 72-73
    take small steps, 66-67
Positive Thinking, chapter six, 75-90

    challenge negative beliefs/thoughts, 78-85
    chapter overview, 89-90
    cognitive therapy, 85-86
    core beliefs, 76-78
    exercise one, 77
    power of visualization, 87-88
    question and answer, 88-89
    table I, II, III, IV, 81,82,83,84

Purposeful Living, chapter eight, 103-111
    chapter overview, 111
    credit card therapy, 104
    finding your purpose, 105-106
    living with purpose, 107-108
    purpose takes practice, 108-109
    question and answer, 109-111
    when your purpose finds you, 106-107

Robert Lipkin, 19-20

Rutgers University, 45

sailboat, 42

Sam Walton, 66

The next step, chapter 10, 123-130
    chapter overview, 130
    creating the big plan, 124-125
    question and answer, 129-130
    signs you need a break, 125-127
    teaching others, 127-129